HSPT®

Practice Questions

HSPT® Practice Tests and Exam Review
for the High School Placement Test
[2nd Edition]

Mometrix
TEST PREPARATION

Written and edited by Matthew Bowling

Printed in the United States of America

This paper meets the requirements of ANSI/NISO Z39.48-1992 (Permanence of Paper).

ISBN 13: 978-1-5167-2736-0
ISBN 10: 1-5167-2736-3

DEAR FUTURE EXAM SUCCESS STORY

First of all, **THANK YOU** for purchasing Mometrix study materials!

Second, congratulations! You are one of the few determined test-takers who are committed to doing whatever it takes to excel on your exam. **You have come to the right place.** We developed these practice tests with one goal in mind: to deliver you the best possible approximation of the questions you will see on test day.

Standardized testing is one of the biggest obstacles on your road to success, which only increases the importance of doing well in the high-pressure, high-stakes environment of test day. Your results on this test could have a significant impact on your future, and these practice tests will give you the repetitions you need to build your familiarity and confidence with the test content and format to help you achieve your full potential on test day.

Your success is our success

We would love to hear from you! If you would like to share the story of your exam success or if you have any questions or comments in regard to our products, please contact us at **800-673-8175** or **support@mometrix.com**.

Thanks again for your business and we wish you continued success!

Sincerely,
The Mometrix Test Preparation Team

TABLE OF CONTENTS

HSPT Practice Test #1

Reading—Comprehension

Refer to the following for questions 1–8:

PARENTING STYLES

When a newborn cries throughout the night, parents can feel at a loss. If they turn to expert advice, they find that even experts disagree on the best solution. The two most popular techniques could not be more contradictory: One encourages parents to let the infant cry himself to sleep. The other encourages "co-sleeping," or letting the infant sleep in the parents' bed.

In the first technique, popularized by Dr. Richard Ferber, parents are encouraged to stick to a strict schedule and teach the infant to adapt. The infant sleeps in a separate room; if he cries, the parents should wait five minutes to check on him. The next time he cries, the parents wait ten minutes. The next time, they wait fifteen. Gradually, the theory goes, the child learns to get back to sleep on his own. This is often called the "cry it out" solution.

At the other end of the spectrum is "attachment parenting." This technique was developed by Dr. William Sears, who argues that the parents should be available to care for the infant if he cries. This technique helps the infant feel that he can rely on his parents to take care of him.

Both sides have their critics. Ferber's technique seems callous and uncaring to some, and Sears's technique seems unsympathetic to sleep-deprived parents. In the end, parents must rely on the only tried and true technique: trial and error.

1. The main purpose of this passage is:

a. To inform readers of two options available to parents of newborns.
b. To convince readers that the "cry it out" method is best.
c. To convince readers that "attachment parenting" is best.
d. To criticize both methods.

2. The meaning nearest to the word co-sleeping is:

a. "cry it out"
b. "attachment parenting"
c. To sleep together
d. To take turns sleeping

3. Which of the following statements can be inferred from the final sentence of the passage?

a. Parents should do what their parents did.
b. Parents should choose one method or the other.
c. Parents should experiment with both methods.
d. Parents should ignore both methods.

4. Which of the following approaches would be part of Dr. Ferber's approach?

a. Teach the infant to get himself to sleep.
b. Teach the infant that he can depend on the parent.
c. Teach the infant to sleep on its back to reduce the risk of Sudden Infant Death Syndrome.
d. Swaddle the infant tightly.

5. The word <u>contradictory</u>, as used in the passage, most nearly means:

a. False
b. Deceitful
c. Conflicting
d. Inexact

6. Which of the following actions would be in keeping with Dr. Sears's approach?

a. Nurse the infant only at certain times of the day and night.
b. Stay close to the infant and attend to his needs.
c. Teach the child sign language so he can communicate from an early age.
d. Reduce the amount of noise in the household.

7. The word <u>callous</u>, as used in the passage, most nearly means:

a. Sensitive
b. Insensitive
c. Doting
d. Flexible

8. Which of the following statements captures the main idea of the passage?

a. Parents should sleep in shifts.
b. Attachment parenting makes children more trusting.
c. Both methods are wrong in different ways.
d. Both methods have faults and strengths.

Refer to the following for questions 9–16:

RECORDING TECHNOLOGY

Though a small number of purists maintain that records of the 1920s and 30s sound better, no one would argue that they sound more complex than those of the 21st Century. Recording technology has evolved into a very <u>intricate</u> process, and the end result often sounds as complex as the technology used to create it. There are three basic stages to the recording process: recording, mixing, and mastering.

Recording involves using microphones to capture the sound of instruments, but it can also involve software-based instruments. <u>Samples</u>, short recorded sounds triggered by a computer or keyboard, and synthesizers have come to replace real instruments in many recordings.

In mixing, each sound from the recording is made to sound as clear as possible. The mixer will choose where to place the sound, either in the left or the right speaker, and whether to add certain textures to the sound, such as <u>reverb</u> or echo, which make some instruments sound further away than others. The mixer can also manipulate the recordings, for instance by making a vocal sound almost robotic.

The last stage, mastering, involves a process called EQ. This is done using a device similar to the treble and bass controls in a car stereo, but it is much more fine-tuned. Mastering can also make the recording louder. In all, modern recordings are highly complex and time-consuming to create, but the end result of this process yields rich sound experiences for the listener.

9. The author of this passage is attempting to:

a. Persuade the reader that recording technology sounded better in the 1920s.
b. Explain some of the complex processes involved in creating 21st Century recordings.
c. Argue that the mixing stage is the most important stage in the recording process.
d. Teach the reader how to record a song.

10. The word <u>intricate</u> most nearly means:

a. Complex
b. Technological
c. Robotic
d. Beautiful

11. According to the passage, which of the following statements is true?

a. EQ is short for "equalization."
b. Only a listener who understands all the stages of the recording process can tell the difference between recordings of the 1920s and today.
c. To perform music well, all musicians have to learn how to record, mix, and master a recording.
d. Changes in technology have greatly impacted the process of recording music.

12. Which of the following statements can be inferred from the last paragraph?

a. Anyone who can work a car stereo can master a record.
b. Mastering is the easiest of the three stages of making a record.
c. EQ can be used to control treble.
d. EQ can make a vocal sound robotic.

13. As used in this passage, the word <u>reverb</u> means:

a. To record something twice
b. Reverse
c. Something that makes instruments sound far away
d. Mixing

14. Which of the following can be inferred from paragraph two?

a. Synthesizers do not sound the same as real instruments.
b. Samples are found inside a microphone.
c. Synthesizers use samples of real instruments.
d. Acoustic guitars are not used in recordings anymore.

15. In this passage, the word <u>samples</u> most nearly refers to:

a. Short recordings of sounds
b. Synthesizers
c. The bass frequencies controlled by an EQ
d. Mixing

16. Which of these statements seems most true based on the passage?

a. Instruments are played during the mixing stage.
b. Synthesizers are used to master a recording.
c. Samples are recorded after the mixing process.
d. Microphones are most often used during the recording process.

Refer to the following for questions 17–24:

CLOUD FORMATION

It is common knowledge that clouds are made of water, but how did the water get there? Why doesn't it fall? Why does the water appear white in its cloud form but not white when we see it on the ground? The knowledge necessary to answer these questions may not be so common after all.

How does it get there? The Sun's heat is the main cause. When it shines on water, the water evaporates and rises into the air in the form of vapor. This vapor is invisible until it reaches higher levels of the atmosphere, where the temperature is much colder. There the water vapor begins to cool down and turn back into tiny droplets of water. If you've ever seen the white condensation that rises above a pot of boiling water, then you've seen a cloud up close.

Why doesn't it fall? It would seem that the water would fall from the sky since it is common knowledge that water is heavier than air. One droplet of water from a cloud, however, is about 10,000 times smaller than a grain of salt. The currents of air in the atmosphere hold these tiny droplets up.

Why is this water white? When you shine a red, green, and yellow light together, they combine to form one white light. Likewise, when sunlight (which contains all the colors of the rainbow) passes through the tiny droplets in a cloud, it scatters all the different colors of light in every direction. It appears as the color white to us because we are seeing all the colors of the rainbow at the same time.

17. The word condensation, as used in this passage, most nearly means:

a. Dry
b. Steam
c. Boiling
d. Atmospheric pressure

18. Which of the following statements can be inferred from this passage?

a. Water can take on different forms depending on the temperature.
b. Clouds are an optical illusion.
c. The effect of gravity's pull on water vapor makes clouds look white.
d. Clouds are made of more than just water.

19. In this passage, the word currents most likely refers to:

a. Electricity
b. Tides
c. Wind
d. Vapor

20. Which of the following statements captures the main idea of the passage?

a. Common knowledge is always wrong.
b. White light is visible when all the colors of the rainbow are present.
c. The properties of clouds are a result of physical causes.
d. The water droplets in clouds are too small to fall.

21. Why does the first paragraph list all the questions the essay will go on to answer?

a. They give a quick overview of the essay's organization.
b. The readers are expected to answer the questions themselves.
c. All good writing should start with questions.
d. These questions form the thesis statement, which should always be phrased as a question.

22. Which of the following statements can be inferred from the third paragraph?

a. Clouds do not fall from the sky because water is always lighter than air.
b. A grain of salt will hang suspended on air currents.
c. Gravity does not pull on objects of such a small size.
d. For an object as small as the droplets in a cloud, air pressure is stronger than gravity.

23. According to the passage, which of the following statements is true?

a. Clouds turn into rain when air currents disappear.
b. Tiny droplets of water cause sunlight to scatter in every direction.
c. Water is not white on the ground because sunlight cannot pass through it.
d. Boiling water is the primary cause of air currents.

24. The author states that water vapor turns back into tiny droplets of water because:

a. Sunlight is stronger at higher layers of the atmosphere.
b. The cold temperature causes the water vapor to change form.
c. Air currents cause the droplets of water to separate from the water vapor.
d. When the water vapor scatters sunlight, it frees the tiny droplets of water.

Refer to the following for questions 25–32:

ALCIBIADES

Alcibiades, born in Athens, Greece, around 450 B.C., was a man of great influence. As a child, he refused to play the flute because he thought it made him look unattractive, and the flute fell out of favor with Athenian youth. As an adult, when he argued that Athens should attack Sicily, the Athenians followed him into a disastrous battle.

Alcibiades switched allegiances several times during the war between Athens and Sparta. He betrayed Athens by forming an alliance with its enemies, the Spartans, whom he led to several successful battles against the Athenians. He was exiled from Sparta for having an inappropriate relationship with the wife of the king, and he went into exile in Persia, enemy of both Athens and Sparta. There Alcibiades allied himself with a local governor, or satrap, whom he helped plot against both Athens and Sparta. Eventually, the Athenians allowed him to return home, where he led several victories against the Spartans. After a defeat, however, Alcibiades was exiled again.

He fled to one of his castles on the coast, where by coincidence he had a view of both the Spartan and Athenian fleets. When he tried to warn the Athenians of the Spartans' superior position, he was ignored. The Athenians suffered a devastating defeat that gave Sparta the upper hand in the war.

According to one account, Alcibiades was murdered in 404 B.C. because he was living with a woman, and her brothers burned his house down to protect her honor. Another account claims that Alcibiades was killed by order of the king of Sparta.

25. What is the main topic of the first paragraph?

a. Alcibiades' influence over his contemporaries
b. Alcibiades' childhood
c. Alcibiades' musicianship
d. Alcibiades' role in the attack of Sicily

26. <u>Satrap</u> is a word meaning:

a. A Greek warrior
b. A Persian leader
c. A traitor
d. Someone from Sparta

27. Which is the true reason Alcibiades was murdered?

a. He violated a code of honor in the community where he lived.
b. He was seen as a threat to the Spartan leaders.
c. We don't know; history has preserved conflicting accounts of his death.
d. He was murdered because he was a traitor.

28. The word <u>allegiances</u> most nearly means:

a. Loyalty
b. Influence
c. Adultery
d. Inhabitants of the Allegheny Mountains

29. Which of the following statements accurately explains why Alcibiades fled to his castle on the coast?

a. So he could see the Spartan and Athenian fleets.
b. So he could spy on the satrap.
c. Because he had been exiled from Athens.
d. Because he wanted to be able to communicate with both Athens and Sparta.

30. What is the main purpose of this passage?

a. To inform the reader about the life of Alcibiades and the war between Athens and Sparta.
b. To persuade the reader that Alcibiades was a victim of conspiracies.
c. To prove that Alcibiades used his relationship with Sparta and Persia to gather information for Athens.
d. To prove that history is never a fully accurate account of the past.

31. The author says that Alcibiades "allied himself" with the Persian satrap, which most nearly means:

a. He spied on him.
b. He had an inappropriate relationship with his wife.
c. He betrayed him.
d. He became his friend and confidant.

32. Which statement best captures the main idea of this passage?

a. Alcibiades offended the king of Sparta by having an affair with his wife.
b. Alcibiades switched allegiances many times during the war.
c. Alcibiades wanted to become king.
d. The Athenians should have listened to Alcibiades when he warned them of the position of the Spartan fleets.

Refer to the following for questions 33–40:

QUANTUM WEIRDNESS

Imagine trying to play a game of basketball in a world without cause and effect. You could throw the ball but you couldn't predict what would happen next. It might pass right through the backboard or disappear for a moment and reappear in the hands of the other team's point guard.

While such a world sounds unimaginably bizarre, the activity it describes is not altogether different from the activity physicists see when they look at particles on the "subatomic level"— the level of existence that is smaller than the electrons, protons, and neutrons that make up atoms. Physicists call this the "quantum realm" and what they discover down there is that particles come in and out of existence without any clear cause. An electron can materialize in one place and then in another, apparently without having to pass through the space in between.

Physicists who are excited by what goes on in the quantum realm are always looking for ways in which our world, the world of basketballs and human bodies, behaves similarly to the quantum world. Some have proposed that brain cells act like quantum particles and that a thought can resemble an uncaused event. Other physicists caution against getting too carried away. They have shown that large-scale objects cancel out quantum weirdness. In a basketball, there may be some weird quantum properties, but they are only detectable on a scale of about 10^{-34} meters. This is a very small number, having thirty-three zeroes between the decimal and the one.

Physicists have largely ruled out finding quantum behavior in objects larger than an electron, which is billions and billions of times smaller than a basketball.

33. What is the main purpose of this passage?

a. To prove that the human brain shows weird quantum properties.
b. To prove that all objects are made of atoms.
c. To inform the reader of the unusual properties of atoms that physicists have discovered.
d. To demonstrate the physics of a basketball game.

34. Physicists are scientists who study:

a. Physics
b. Physiology
c. Subatomic particles
d. Physical education

35. According to the third paragraph, the number 10^{-34} is best described as:

a. A minuscule number
b. An enormous number
c. The number of molecules in a basketball
d. The distance between a proton and an electron

36. Which of the following statements can be inferred from this passage?

a. All physicists believe that basketballs can disappear.
b. Some physicists have argued that brain cells cannot act like quantum particles.
c. No physicists believe in cause and effect anymore.
d. Some physicists deny the existence of subatomic particles.

37. The word subatomic most nearly refers to:

a. The world found at the level of molecules.
b. The cells that make up the human brain.
c. The world smaller than the atom.
d. The molecules that make up a basketball.

38. According to the passage, an electron is:

a. A unit of measurement.
b. An electrical cloud that surrounds a molecule.
c. A subatomic particle.
d. One of the elements listed on the periodic table.

39. Reread the first three sentences of paragraph 3. Which one of the following statements most closely captures the author's meaning in this sentence, "Other physicists caution against getting too carried away"?

a. Some physicists think this interpretation goes too far.
b. Some physicists think this interpretation is not creative enough.
c. Some physicists think this interpretation is correct.
d. Some physicists think others are lying in order to get attention.

40. It can be inferred from this passage that:

a. All physicists agree about the meaning of quantum weirdness.
b. Physicists don't know whether quantum weirdness is cancelled out in large objects.
c. Physicists have observed that the quantum world and the visible world are very different.
d. Physicists think that the quantum world is not real.

Reading—Vocabulary

Refer to the following for questions 1–22:

Select the answer that is closest in meaning to the underlined portion.

1. The painful slight

a. Daydream
b. Passive
c. Formality
d. Insult

2. The mortified clerk

a. Cold
b. Embarrassed
c. Drowsy
d. Excited

3. The fortified perimeter

a. Boundary
b. Distance
c. Intimacy
d. Jewel

4. The bear slumbered in its cave.

a. hunted
b. fed
c. slept
d. explored

5. The company instantly agreed to the terms of the contract.

a. reluctantly
b. eventually
c. immediately
d. definitely

6. A persistent cough

a. Ongoing
b. Loud
c. Hollow
d. Contagious

7. The disadvantaged child

a. Deprived
b. Victorious
c. Adopted
d. Gifted

8. She was doubtful whether the plan would work.

a. uncertain
b. panicked
c. pondering
d. indifferent

9. Time for recuperation

a. Healing
b. Replacement
c. Drinking
d. Discipline

10. She kept her house tidy.

a. furnished
b. warm
c. locked
d. neat

11. She felt intense anguish when her parents divorced.

a. loneliness
b. confusion
c. anger
d. sorrow

12. His faltering defense

a. Hesitating
b. Proud
c. Decisive
d. Impractical

13. The volatile chemical

a. Harmless
b. Inert
c. Small
d. Explosive

14. A shrill tone

a. High-pitched
b. Low
c. Punitive
d. Soft

15. A hypocritical politician

a. Confident
b. Persuasive
c. Authoritative
d. Insincere

16. A functioning customer service department is <u>vital</u> to the company's survival.

a. lively
b. essential
c. optional
d. trivial

17. The audience applauded after the woman <u>concluded</u> her presentation.

a. delivered
b. prepared
c. attended
d. finished

18. Different species of birds <u>migrate</u> to warmer climates, escaping the fridged temperatures of winter.

a. generate
b. hibernate
c. integrate
d. relocate

19. Although the disease gave the patient a <u>formidable</u> battle for her life, she survived despite the odds.

a. approachable
b. intimidating
c. manageable
d. trivial

20. After the student revised his essay multiple times, his assertions became clearer and more <u>coherent</u>.

a. ambiguous
b. disjointed
c. fragmented
d. logical

21. Her prediction was <u>accurate</u>.

a. correct
b. false
c. funny
d. planned

22. She is having <u>difficulties</u> with her new computer.

a. experiences
b. solutions
c. pleasures
d. problems

Language

1. Select the sentence with an error in usage, punctuation, or grammar. If no errors are found, choose the last option.

a. Wind always blows from areas of higher to lower atmospheric pressure.
b. Tillie, the German shepherd was always the first one to know when Dad got home.
c. Throughout his testimonial, the witness cleaned his glasses with his tie.
d. No mistake.

2. Select the sentence with an error in usage, punctuation, or grammar. If no errors are found, choose the last option.

a. Though I had only met him recently, I felt as though I had long known Jon.
b. There were very few people left on the streets after sundown.
c. There are over 600 species of bacteria living in the human mouth at any time.
d. No mistake.

3. Select the sentence with an error in usage, punctuation, or grammar. If no errors are found, choose the last option.

a. The world's population, growing at 4.2 births every second and dropping by 1.7 deaths.
b. Woodrow Wilson said, "You are here to enrich the world and you impoverish yourself if you forget that errand."
c. The word "infant" originally meant "not speaking," and the word "nice" meant "ignorant."
d. No mistake.

4. Select the sentence with an error in usage, punctuation, or grammar. If no errors are found, choose the last option.

a. The highest point on Earth is 29,028 feet, at the top of Mt. Everest, and the lowest is 36,198 feet below sea level, in the Mariana Trench near the Philippines.
b. The Guggenheim Museum in Manhattan was designed by renowned architect Frank Lloyd Wright.
c. The great Aswan Dam was built in 1902 in Egypt to help farmers irrigate their crops and to prevent his fields from flooding.
d. No mistake.

5. Select the sentence with an error in usage, punctuation, or grammar. If no errors are found, choose the last option.

a. The Fourth of July fireworks display always upsets our neighbors' dogs.
b. The field of Medical Geography studies the ways a disease spreads throughout a region, the field was created in 1854 when a physician mapped out all the cholera cases in London and connected many of them to a single contaminated water pump.
c. The equinoxes take place on the 21st of March and September.
d. No mistake.

6. Select the sentence with an error in usage, punctuation, or grammar. If no errors are found, choose the last option.

a. The electrical outlet had a long charred trail above it.
b. The coliseum in Rome was once quarried to supply raw materials for nearby churches.
c. The children were instructed to hold hands until we arrived at the park.
d. No mistake.

7. Select the sentence with an error in usage, punctuation, or grammar. If no errors are found, choose the last option.

a. The governor wanted to legalize bottle rockets again to keep people from crossing state lines to purchase fireworks.
b. When Sumo wrestlers lift their legs and stomp the floor, their movements reflect an ancient Shinto ritual for driving away demons.
c. There is many healthy vegetables in my grandmother's garden.
d. No mistake.

8. Select the sentence with an error in usage, punctuation, or grammar. If no errors are found, choose the last option.

a. Studies show that adolescents who believe they will die before the age of 35 are more likely to engage in dangerous, risk-taking behavior.
b. The Wardrops' estate had fallen into disrepair until they attracted the interest of the local historical preservation society.
c. Students who try to remember their homework assignments instead of writing them down rarely remembers everything correctly.
d. No mistake.

9. Select the sentence with an error in usage, punctuation, or grammar. If no errors are found, choose the last option.

a. Some viruses are very slow-acting and stay embedded in their hosts' cells.
b. Some argued that many people would be unprepared for the switch from analog to digital television signals.
c. Solids, liquids, and gasses are not separate types of matter, but three separately stages, like ice, water, and vapor.
d. No mistake.

10. Select the sentence with an error in usage, punctuation, or grammar. If no errors are found, choose the last option.

a. Skunks are "crepuscular," meaning they are most active at twilight.
b. Roy pasted glow-in-the-dark pictures of all nine planets in our solar system on his ceiling they turned green when he turned off the light.
c. While he was emperor of Rome, Tiberius did not live there; instead, he lived on an island and sent his orders by lantern, using a code called "semaphore."
d. No mistake.

11. Select the sentence with an error in usage, punctuation, or grammar. If no errors are found, choose the last option.

a. Rachel named her new pet blowfish "Carl" because that was the name of the clerk who sold it to her at the pet store.
b. In North Weymouth, Massachusetts, Pilgrim Congregational Church allows members to bring their pets to the church service.
c. Pete was well known for his impersonations.
d. No mistake.

12. Select the sentence with an error in usage, punctuation, or grammar. If no errors are found, choose the last option.

a. Orange Pekoe is my favorite tea.
b. Only two people showed up to the garage sale all day.
c. Not one of the tomato plants survived the freeze.
d. No mistake.

13. Select the sentence with an error in usage, punctuation, or grammar. If no errors are found, choose the last option.

a. Norma included a handheld vacuum cleaner in the picnic basket.
b. No one was injured when the car slipped out of gear and rolled downhill into the lake.
c. No one were allowed in the restaurant until the police had left.
d. No mistake.

14. Select the sentence with an error in usage, punctuation, or grammar. If no errors are found, choose the last option.

a. The last time I went to Nevada, I get a terrible sunburn.
b. Martin Waldseemueller is remembered for his publication of a map in 1507 that was the first to use the name "America."
c. No one seemed readier to leave the ceremony than the guest of honor.
d. No mistake.

15. Select the sentence with an error in usage, punctuation, or grammar. If no errors are found, choose the last option.

a. Mediterranean fishermen kills an octopus by biting it behind each eye.
b. Maurice and Robin Gibb, two of the members of the Bee Gees, are twin brothers.
c. Fortunately, no one arrived in time to see the enormous mess I'd made in the kitchen.
d. No mistake.

16. Select the sentence with an error in usage, punctuation, or grammar. If no errors are found, choose the last option.

a. Many hotels throw out linens after they are a month old, some have started donating them to those in need.
b. Luxembourg is only 51 miles from north to south and, at its widest, 35 miles across from east to west.
c. Atoms combine with other atoms to form molecules.
d. No mistake.

17. Select the sentence with an error in usage, punctuation, or grammar. If no errors are found, choose the last option.

a. The United States is allowed to lease Guantanamo Bay from Cuba for a naval base as part of an agreement that dates back to 1902.
b. The US did not officially have time zones until Congress' passed the Standard Time Act of 1918.
c. The stinging tentacles of anemones are called nematocysts.
d. No mistake.

18. Select the sentence with an error in usage, punctuation, or grammar. If no errors are found, choose the last option.

a. No one at the table even noticed that the man was choking until the waiter rushed over to perform the Heimlich maneuver on him.
b. The committee members couldn't hardly conceal their enthusiasm for the new measure.
c. Nero, Emperor of Rome, is believed to be responsible for a fire that burnt much of that city.
d. No mistake.

19. Select the sentence with an error in usage, punctuation, or grammar. If no errors are found, choose the last option.

a. Much whispering broke loose in the chapel when the groom appeared with a black eye.
b. No one mentioned George's job loss during dinner.
c. After Michael worked three shifts on Saturday and slept all day Sunday.
d. No mistake.

20. Select the sentence with an error in usage, punctuation, or grammar. If no errors are found, choose the last option.

a. L-Taurine is an amino acid that is said to help with depression.
b. On the equinox, night and day is the same length.
c. Joel should have secured the cage better because the dog got out of the kennel in mid-flight.
d. No mistake.

21. Select the sentence with an error in usage, punctuation, or grammar. If no errors are found, choose the last option.

a. Jesse finished the crossword puzzle in twenty minutes.
b. It is unlikely that we will see much of the money from the settlement after the lawyers and court fees are paid.
c. It is not correct to call people from Wales, Scotland, or Northern Ireland "English" because they are not from England, they are Welsh, Scottish, or Irish.
d. No mistake.

22. Select the sentence with an error in usage, punctuation, or grammar. If no errors are found, choose the last option.

a. It is estimated that one million people died during the potato famine in Ireland from 1845-1850, while another two million immigrated to other countries.
b. Pete always mow the yard with a can of Raid wasp spray in his pocket.
c. The jacket was nice, but the sleeves were too short.
d. No mistake.

23. Select the sentence with an error in usage, punctuation, or grammar. If no errors are found, choose the last option.

a. The radio station broke a record by playing "Stairway to Heaven" ninety times in a row.
b. The pledge drive lasted a week.
c. The post office clerk asked whether the heavy package I'd ordered contained rocks or dumb bells?
d. No mistake.

24. Select the sentence with an error in usage, punctuation, or grammar. If no errors are found, choose the last option.

a. The population of the US rose by two million People in between 2008 and 2009, reaching 305,529,237.
b. Scientists think that Christopher Columbus died from a bacterial infection that he caught from the parrots aboard his ship.
c. Some corn crops create their own insecticides.
d. No mistake.

25. Select the sentence with an error in usage, punctuation, or grammar. If no errors are found, choose the last option.

a. Very little life can be found above 27,000 feet, and no animals are known to live below 35,800 feet below sea level.
b. Saturn's rings are invisible when they face Earth edge-on because they are not thick enough to be seen through a telescope.
c. The record for the world's lowest temperature is held by Siberia, where temperatures reached ninety degrees below zero on February 6 1933.
d. No mistake.

26. Select the sentence with an error in usage, punctuation, or grammar. If no errors are found, choose the last option.

a. William Bryant was the first african-American to serve as a federal judge.
b. The so-called railroad worm glows red on its head and greenish-yellow along its eleven segments.
c. In snow storms, cattle huddle so closely together that they are more likely to die of suffocation than freeze to death.
d. No mistake.

27. Select the sentence with an error in usage, punctuation, or grammar. If no errors are found, choose the last option.

a. Belgium, The Netherlands, and Luxemburg is known as the "low countries" because of their low elevation.
b. The restaurant was sued for not being accessible to the handicapped.
c. The North Magnetic Pole is moving at a rate of about 25 miles per year.
d. No mistake.

28. Select the sentence with an error in usage, punctuation, or grammar. If no errors are found, choose the last option.

a. In between performances, the musicians paced backstage on their cell phones.
b. In 1582, Pope Gregory declared October 5 to be changed to October 15 to correct the calendar.
c. I was not the first person to compliment Ira on his new glasses.
d. No mistake.

29. Select the sentence with an error in usage, punctuation, or grammar. If no errors are found, choose the last option.

a. I stood in line for the restroom for nearly fifteen minutes.
b. Nebraska is the only state in the US that doesn't have two legislative houses.
c. Nate seemed uninterested in the celebration he was texting on his cell phone.
d. No mistake.

30. Select the sentence with an error in usage, punctuation, or grammar. If no errors are found, choose the last option.

a. In Native American societies that practice the "potlatch," individuals gain status by giving gifts.
b. My grandfather went to the driving range the day after Christmas to try out the golf clubs we bought for him.
c. I spent five hours trying to writes the speech I was supposed to give the next day.
d. No mistake.

31. Select the sentence with an error in usage, punctuation, or grammar. If no errors are found, choose the last option.

a. I drank the last of the milk from the refrigerator.
b. The Hutterites' origins date back to the 16th Century in Europe.
c. Hours after the football game ended, traffic remained backed up.
d. No mistake.

32. Select the sentence with an error in usage, punctuation, or grammar. If no errors are found, choose the last option.

a. Halfway to work, I realized I'd left my wallet at my House.
b. The pressure of a gas rises as the temperature increases.
c. Gertrude Stein once called Ezra Pound "the village explainer," and she added, "Very useful if you happen to be a village; if not, not."
d. No mistake.

33. Select the sentence with an error in usage, punctuation, or grammar. If no errors are found, choose the last option.

a. From the airplane, the two islands looked exactly like a lowercase "i."
b. For a few days after the accident, I couldnt look from side to side.
c. David Copperfield is widely considered to be Charles Dickens' best work.
d. No mistake.

34. Select the sentence with an error in usage, punctuation, or grammar. If no errors are found, choose the last option.

a. Few people seemed enthusiastic about the three-day bike tour after the weather hitted the triple digits.
b. Except for a one-hundred mile stretch in Panama, the Pan-American Highway stretches all the way from Fairbanks, Alaska, to Buenos Aires, Argentina.
c. Every year, Aunt Florence's Christmas fudge block arrived in the mail and had to be divided into equal chunks for each person in the family.
d. No mistake.

35. Select the sentence with an error in usage, punctuation, or grammar. If no errors are found, choose the last option.

a. Evan had a hard time getting back into his sleep schedule after school started.
b. Eileen's poncho got caught in the elevator door.
c. In downtown Enterprise, Alabama, one can find a monument in honor of the boll weevil.
d. No mistake.

36. Select the sentence with an error in usage, punctuation, or grammar. If no errors are found, choose the last option.

a. I had to wake Dorie to keep her from snoring during the ceremony.
b. After eight hours on the airplane, all the infants onboard started crying.
c. Elephants take mud baths to protect themselves against parasites sunburn and overheating.
d. No mistake.

37. Select the sentence with an error in usage, punctuation, or grammar. If no errors are found, choose the last option.

a. Angela earned three credits toward her high school diploma by doing extra credit work.
b. Collin's uncle ran an after-school program called "Rock Climbers Rule," a name that Collin suggested.
c. Christa's new cell phone had a laser pointer.
d. No mistake.

38. Select the sentence with an error in usage, punctuation, or grammar. If no errors are found, choose the last option.

a. Caves are formed when underground water comes into contact with a material it can dissolve, such as limestone.
b. Carole researched the energy efficiency, of several brands of toaster.
c. Beverly came in third place despite having the lead for most of the race.
d. No mistake.

39. Select the sentence with an error in usage, punctuation, or grammar. If no errors are found, choose the last option.

a. Mrs. Bellamy sang in a high Soprano voice that always stood out from the rest of the choir.
b. Because he was too short, Cameron was not allowed on the roller coaster.
c. Joseph Smith founded the Mormon religion after discovering gold plates buried in a hill near his home.
d. No mistake.

40. Select the sentence with an error in usage, punctuation, or grammar. If no errors are found, choose the last option.

a. Ashley's application for a student loan was denied, but she still planned to attend the university.
b. Betsy packed her toothpaste toothbrush and dental floss in a plastic bag.
c. Arteries carry more oxygen, and veins carry more carbon dioxide.
d. No mistake.

41. Select the sentence with an error in usage, punctuation, or grammar. If no errors are found, choose the last option.

a. An isotope of a hydrogen atom has the same number of protons as a regular hydrogen atom, but a different number of neutrons.
b. Alice said, "I didn't invite him to the party in the first place."
c. Alfred Hitchcock was a master at creating suspenseful films.
d. No mistake.

42. Select the sentence with an error in usage, punctuation, or grammar. If no errors are found, choose the last option.

a. After the crowd left, Everett picked up all the plates and cups.
b. A radioactive element releases particles because its nucleus is not bound together in a stable way.
c. Dolores asked whether I mights like to study piano with her.
d. No mistake.

43. Select the sentence with an error in spelling. If no errors are found, choose the last option.

a. The yellow flowers are daffodils, and the orange ones are tiger lilies.
b. The bus arrived earlier then scheduled.
c. After lightning struck the house, the television looked blurry.
d. No mistake.

44. Select the sentence with an error in spelling. If no errors are found, choose the last option.

a. The black cat had one white side where it rubbed against the wet paint in the garrage.
b. Mike shined his flashlight into the crawl space, and a centipede crawled out.
c. The farmer had to go into the fields during the rain to shut off the irrigation system.
d. No mistake.

45. Select the sentence with an error in spelling. If no errors are found, choose the last option.

a. The ambulance sirens in Europe sound two notes tuned to an interval called a "tritone."
b. Grandmother was surprised to find that her two-year-old granddaughter had secretly packed an open tube of paint in her clean clothes.
c. The word "piano" comes from the Italian word for "soft."
d. No mistake.

46. Select the sentence with an error in spelling. If no errors are found, choose the last option.

a. The mellotron is an instrument that looks like a piano, but it uses prerecorded tapes of flutes and cellos instead of piano strings.
b. Joel said the lasagna was as easy to eat as the soul of his shoe.
c. Whenever it rains, doors are harder to close because the vapor in the atmosphere gets in the wood's pores and causes them to expand.
d. No mistake.

47. Select the sentence with an error in spelling. If no errors are found, choose the last option.

a. Kudzu is an invasive vine that has overgrown seven million acres in the southeastern US
b. When an apple starts to decay, it releases a gas called ethylene, which can trigger decay in nearby apples.
c. My father always asked me to hold his boot while he pulled his foot out.
d. No mistake.

48. Select the sentence with an error in spelling. If no errors are found, choose the last option.

a. The camels at the zoo looked as though they were loosing their fur.
b. Maltodextrin is a food additive that is used in artificial sweeteners for its sweet taste and in salad dressings as a thickening agent.
c. Leo Fender, the creator of Fender guitars, was not a guitar player.
d. No mistake.

49. Select the sentence with an error in spelling. If no errors are found, choose the last option.

a. When my jump rope broke, all of its tiny plastic pieces spilled all over the basketball court.
b. Physicist Stephen Hawking suffers from a disease called ALS, better known as Lou Gehrig's disease.
c. I thought my neice named her hamster after me, until she told me that there was an Uncle Richard in her favorite cartoon.
d. No mistake.

50. Select the sentence with an error in spelling. If no errors are found, choose the last option.

a. The "stroopwafel" is a popular dessert in the Netherlands. It is made of two thin waffles held together by thick caramel syrup.
b. The homework assignment took me all evenning to complete.
c. I thought my bicycle was stolen until I remembered getting a ride home from school.
d. No mistake.

51. Where should the following sentence be placed in the paragraph below?

Examples of these problematic beliefs are statements such as, "Everyone should love me" and "I must never be wrong."

1] Albert Ellis created Rational Emotive Behavioral Therapy in the 1950s. 2] His primary aim was to help people overcome the problematic beliefs that cause them unhappiness. 3] Ellis observed that most negative emotions are due to beliefs that come in the form of commands containing words like "should," "ought," or "must." 4] For instance, someone who is upset because a coworker complained about him to his boss could analyze his response and find that the source of the unpleasant emotion is the belief that "everyone must approve of me."

a. After sentence 1
b. After sentence 2
c. After sentence 3
d. After sentence 4

52. Where should the following sentence be placed in the paragraph below?

Supporters of HFCS, however, point to research that shows no connection to obesity at all.

1] High fructose corn syrup (HFCS) is a sweetener used in many foods and soft drinks. 2] HFCS is created by grinding corn into corn starch, processing the starch to turn it into corn syrup, and then treating it with enzymes to turn it into fructose. 3] The result is a cheap, very sweet syrup that shows up in many of the food and drinks we consume every day, particularly soft drinks. 4] Critics of HFCS cite research that seems to prove that it increases obesity. 5] Another controversy concerns the use of the phrase "natural ingredients" on products containing HFCS. 6] Supporters say that it can be called natural because it comes from corn, but critics argue that after all the processing it is put through, it is no longer appropriate to call it "natural."

a. After sentence 1
b. After sentence 2
c. After sentence 3
d. After sentence 4

53. Choose the word or words that best fill the blank.

The members of the fraternity were accused of hazing the incoming freshmen, ______ none of the freshmen testified against them.

a. but
b. so
c. because
d. and

54. Choose the word or words that best fill the blank.

"Detasseling," or sending groups of teenagers into corn fields to pluck the pollinating tassels from corn stalks, has become a rite of passage in many agricultural communities in the Midwest ____ for many teens, it is their first paying job.

a. though,
b. because,
c. but,
d. nonetheless,

55. Choose the word or words that best fill the blank.

We felt proud that our garden produced zucchinis the size of an adult human leg, ___ we didn't realize they taste best when harvested early while still small.

a. but
b. instead
c. nor
d. while

56. Choose the sentence that is correct and most clearly written.

a. Her five kittens under the back steps the gray cat hid.
b. Under the back steps her five kittens were hidden by the gray cat.
c. The gray cat hid her five kittens under the back steps.
d. The five kittens were hidden under the back steps by the gray cat.

57. Choose the sentence that is correct and most clearly written.

a. The kitchen was flooded by the broken pipe before the tiles starting to bulge.
b. After the broken pipe flooded the kitchen, the tiles started to bulge.
c. Before the tiles started to bulge, the kitchen is flooded by the broken pipe.
d. The tiles started to bulge but not until after the kitchen was flooding by the broken pipe.

58. Choose the sentence that is correct and most clearly written.

a. Jim bailed out the flooded basement by hand.
b. By hand the flooded basement was bailing out by Jim.
c. The flooded basement was bails out by hand by Jim.
d. Bailed out by Jim by hand was the flooded basement.

59. Which sentence does *not* belong in the following paragraph?

1] There are many uses for recycled tires. 2] Industries can use them as a fuel source because they can burn for a long time. 3] Playgrounds can shred them and use them beneath jungle gyms to protect children if they should fall. 4] Accidents on playgrounds are far more common when there is no adult supervision. 5] Recycled tires can also be used by manufacturers of shoe soles and rubber boots.

a. Sentence 2
b. Sentence 3
c. Sentence 4
d. Sentence 5

60. Which sentence does *not* belong in the following paragraph?

1] "Alternative country," better known as "alt-country" has its roots in the music of Johnny Cash, Neil Young, and Bob Dylan, who combined country and rock music. 2] Bob Dylan's best work would have to be the albums *Blonde on Blonde* and *Highway 61 Revisited*. 3] Alt-Country can easily be distinguished from country music because it combines elements of other genres, such as rock and even experimental music. 4] Though artists like the Byrds and the Flying Burrito Brothers successfully combined country music with other genres of music in the 1960s and 1970s, alt-country was first labeled in the 1990s when bands like Uncle Tupelo and Whiskeytown started creating a new sound that sounded like country music, but it defied clear categorization.

a. Sentence 2
b. Sentence 3
c. Sentence 4
d. Sentence 5

Verbal Skills

1. Cordial means the *opposite* of:

a. Inhospitable
b. Sterile
c. Beloved
d. Entwined

2. Which word does NOT belong with the others?

a. Furniture
b. Table
c. Desk
d. Chair

3. Mutiny most nearly means:

a. Revolt
b. Measurement
c. Ship
d. Ammunition

4. Which word does NOT belong with the others?

a. Toaster
b. Oven
c. Appliance
d. Coffee maker

5. Which word does NOT belong with the others?

a. Fragrant
b. Ambrosial
c. Aromatic
d. Malodorous

6. Reece was married the month before Lee. Darren got married after Lee. Reece got married after Darren. If the first two statements are true, then the third is:

a. True
b. False
c. Unknown
d. Incomplete

7. Apple is to seed as person is to:

a. Parent
b. Embryo
c. Nourishment
d. Cell

8. Escalate means the *opposite* of:

a. Rise
b. Soar
c. Plummet
d. Increase

9. Potent is the *opposite* of:

a. Concentrated
b. Disillusioned
c. Diligent
d. Weak

10. Subjective is the *opposite* of:

a. Definitive
b. Furtive
c. Objective
d. Restive

11. Which word does NOT belong with the others?

a. Cumulus
b. Cirrus
c. Clouds
d. Stratus

12. Electricity is to outlet as water is to:

a. Plumber
b. Ice
c. Pool
d. Faucet

13. Which word does NOT belong with the others?

a. Quotation marks
b. Punctuation
c. Semicolon
d. Period

14. Agitate most nearly means:

a. Alleviate
b. Confide
c. Approach
d. Disturb

15. Flounder most nearly means:

a. Decay
b. Struggle
c. Grapple
d. Flourish

16. Attest most nearly means:

a. Disprove
b. Abstain
c. Extract
d. Vouch

17. Tasteful means the *opposite* of:

a. Vulgar
b. Delicious
c. Elevated
d. Acute

18. Complete means the *opposite* of:

a. Finish
b. Conclude
c. Begin
d. Done

19. Gianna's birthday is the month before Javier's. Caiden's birthday is after Javier's. Gianna's birthday is after Caiden's. If the first two statements are true, then the third statement is:

a. True
b. False
c. Unknown

20. Commence most nearly means:

a. Begin
b. Progress
c. Finish
d. Comment

21. Optimum most nearly means:

a. Ideal
b. Visual
c. Silent
d. Temporal

22. Candor most nearly means:

a. Honesty
b. Evasive
c. Reticence
d. Cautious

23. Esther drove the same distance as Marcus. Lee drove twice as far as Marcus. Esther drove farther than Lee. If the first two statements are true, then the third is:

a. True
b. False
c. Unknown
d. An opinion

24. Annoying means the *opposite* of:

a. Maddening
b. Pleasing
c. Frustrating
d. Irritating

25. Abrasive most nearly means:

a. Irritating
b. Voracious
c. Gentle
d. Furtive

26. Marry most nearly means:

a. Jolly
b. Resolve
c. Divorce
d. Join

27. Pledge means the *opposite* of:

a. Breach
b. Compromise
c. Vivid
d. Sanction

28. Which word does NOT belong with the others?

a. Chair
b. Couch
c. Bed
d. Furniture

29. Shun means the *opposite* of:

a. Return
b. Embrace
c. Manipulate
d. Retract

30. Liable most nearly means:

a. Irresponsible
b. Responsible
c. Unable
d. Ineligible

31. Which word does NOT belong with the others?

a. Gasoline
b. Inflammable
c. Ignitable
d. Combustible

32. Which word does NOT belong with the others?

a. Poodle
b. Boxer
c. Cardinal
d. Labrador

33. The football game lasted an hour longer than the baseball game. The soccer game was an hour longer than the football game. The baseball game took longer than the soccer game. If the first two statements are true, then the third is:

a. True
b. False
c. Unknown

34. Mindful means the *opposite* of:

a. Inattentive
b. Explosive
c. Knowledgeable
d. Telepathic

35. Intermission is to drama as plant is to:

a. Compliment
b. Constellation
c. Habitat
d. Memorabilia

36. Temperature is to heat as pound is to:

a. Weight
b. Height
c. Measurement
d. Heavy

37. Brett left basketball practice after Dane. Dane left practice before John. John left practice before Brett. If the first two statements are true, then the third statement is:

a. True
b. False
c. Unknown

38. Ice is to skate as water is to:

a. Lake
b. Wash
c. Drink
d. Swim

39. Exercise is fitness as:

a. Wing is to bird
b. Horse is to saddle
c. Laziness is to activity
d. Study is to knowledge

40. Cognizant most nearly means:

a. Belligerent
b. Aware
c. Indifferent
d. Honorable

41. Opaque most nearly means:

a. Crystal
b. Clear
c. Dark
d. Memorial

42. Solitary most nearly means:

a. Single
b. Solid
c. Sturdy
d. Stoic

43. Otis caught more beads than Steve at Mardi Gras. Steve got as many beads as Carrie. Carrie got fewer beads than Otis. If the first two statements are true, then the third is:

a. True
b. False
c. Unknown
d. Redundant

44. Metal Leather sold far fewer records than The Animal Instincts. The Gang Mentality sold ten times the records The Animal Instincts sold. The Gang Mentality sold fewer records than Metal Leather. If the first two statements are true, then the third is:

a. True
b. False
c. Unknown
d. Incomplete

45. Almost means the *opposite* of:

a. Nearly
b. Exactly
c. Practically
d. Roughly

46. Dorine won more awards than Heather won at the competition. Alice won fewer awards than Dorine. Heather won fewer awards than Alice. If the first two statements are true, then the third is:

a. True
b. False
c. Uncertain

47. Rocco is taller than Ashley. Brian is shorter than Ashley. Rocco is taller than Brian. If the first two statements are true, then the third is:

a. True
b. False
c. Unknown

48. Which word does NOT belong with the others?

a. Facilitate
b. Obstruct
c. Block
d. Barricade

49. Espionage is to discreet as kindling is to:

a. Grotesque
b. Majestic
c. Novelty
d. Ominous

50. Which word does NOT belong with the others?

a. Private
b. Doctor
c. Corporal
d. Sergeant

51. Pantomime most nearly means:

a. Mimic
b. Clothes
c. Jester
d. Book

52. Cry is to sadness as:

a. Fear is to function
b. Yell is to anger
c. Happiness is to smile
d. Doubt is to confusion

53. Monica scored higher on the test than Ray. Ray outscored Juliet. Juliet scored higher on the test than Monica. If the first two statements are true, then the third is:

a. True
b. False
c. Unknown

54. General means the *opposite* of:

a. Military
b. Decisive
c. Abstract
d. Particular

55. Which word does NOT belong with the others?

a. Dentist
b. Professional
c. Lawyer
d. Dermatologist

56. Enliven means the *opposite* of:

a. Depress
b. Imagine
c. Accost
d. Refrain

57. Robust means the *opposite* of:

a. Rotund
b. Distracted
c. Sickly
d. animated

58. Expend is the *opposite* of:

a. Conserve
b. Disburse
c. Rescind
d. Divulge

59. Which word does NOT belong with the others?

a. Delaware
b. Puerto Rico
c. Hawaii
d. California

60. Which word does NOT belong with the others?

a. Elementary
b. School
c. Junior high
d. College

Quantitative Skills

1. Which number belongs inside the last triangle? Hint: Use operations with the outside numbers to generate the inside number.

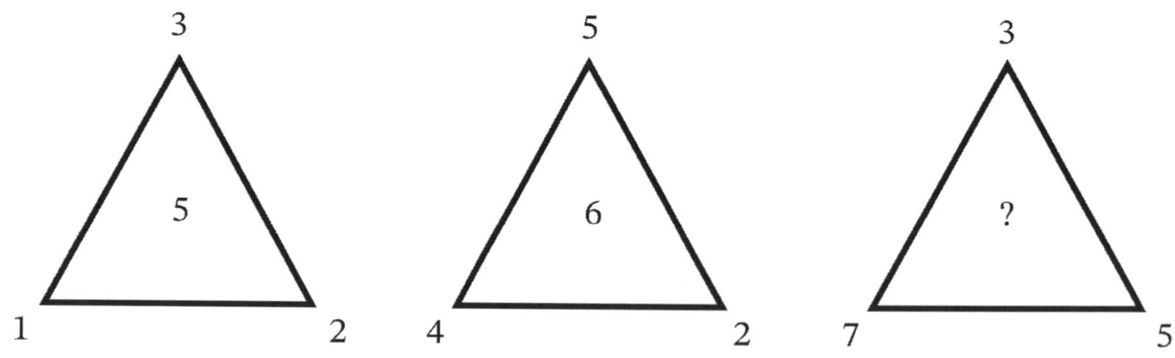

a. 6
b. 8
c. 9
d. 12

2. Examine (I), (II), and (III) and select the best answer.

(I) An integer greater than 4 but less than 6
(II) An integer equal to half of 10
(III) A prime number greater than 3 but less than 7

a. (I) must be equal to (II), but is not necessarily equal to (III).
b. (I) must be equal to both (II) and (III).
c. (I) is not necessarily equal to (II), but (II) must be equal to (III).
d. None of the items is necessarily equal to any of the others.

3. On a number line, point *A* is at −3, point *B* is at 5, and point *C* is at 21. Which of the following statements is correct?

a. Point B is twice as far from point C as it is from point A.
b. Point C is 3 times as far from point A as it is from point B.
c. Point A is more than 5 times as far from point C as it is from point B.
d. Point B is halfway between points A and C.

4. Examine (I), (II), and (III), and select the best answer.

(I) 4^3
(II) 5^2
(III) 3^4

a. (I) $>$ (II) $>$ (III)
b. (I) $>$ (II) $<$ (III)
c. (I) $<$ (II) $<$ (III)
d. (I) $<$ (II) $>$ (III)

5. Which number has no remainder when divided into 250?

a. 5
b. 15
c. 20
d. 30

6. What is the 6th term in the sequence?

113, −226, 452...

a. −3,822
b. −3,800
c. −3,616
d. 3,616

7. Which of the following fractions, when substituted for *x*, makes the statement true?

$$\frac{3}{8} < x < \frac{13}{24}$$

a. $\frac{7}{8}$
b. $\frac{5}{8}$
c. $\frac{5}{12}$
d. $\frac{1}{3}$

8. The sequence is considered ___________.

−4, −6, −8, −10...

a. linear
b. arithmetic
c. quadratic
d. geometric

9. Half of what number is equal to 15% of 70?

a. 20
b. 21
c. 22
d. 23

10. A right triangle has legs of length 5 inches and 6 inches. What can we say about its perimeter?

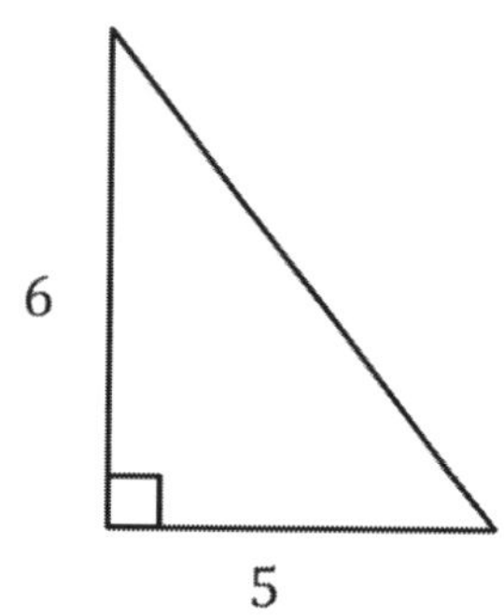

a. The perimeter is between 15 and 16 inches.
b. The perimeter is between 16 and 17 inches.
c. The perimeter is between 17 and 18 inches.
d. The perimeter is between 18 and 19 inches.

11. Two small circles have their centers on a diameter of a large circle. Each small circle touches the large circle at one end of the diameter and they both pass through the center of the large circle, as shown.

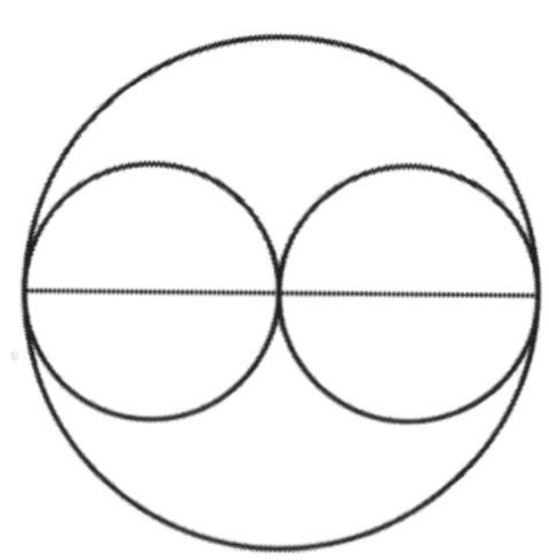

If C_1 is the circumference of the large circle and C_2 is the sum of the circumferences of the small circles, how do C_1 and C_2 compare?

a. $C_1 < C_2$
b. $C_1 > C_2$
c. $C_1 = C_2$
d. The problem provides insufficient information to determine how C_1 and C_2 compare.

12. What is the next term in the sequence?

$$-5, 10, -20, 40, -80, \_\_$$

a. –160
b. –150
c. 150
d. 160

13. Which numeral comes next in the sequence 3, 9, 27, 81, ...?

a. 108
b. 162
c. 243
d. 324

14. Which of the following is greatest?

a. $\frac{4}{5}$ of 80
b. 20% of 20
c. 7% of 1,400
d. $3^{(6-2)}$

15. Which of the following is the greatest?

a. $6 - 2$
b. $-4 - 2$
c. $-4 - (-10)$
d. $11 - 6$

16. Mr. Carver is teaching his students about deductive reasoning and states the premises listed below. Which of these students has reached a valid conclusion?

Premise 1	All primates are mammals.
Premise 2	All lemurs are primates.

a. Mia states, "All primates are lemurs."
b. Carlos states, "All lemurs are mammals."
c. Xavier states, "All whales are mammals."
d. Gavin states, "All monkeys are primates."

17. What number multiplied by 8 is 5 more than 59?

a. 6
b. 7
c. 8
d. 9

18. Which of the following numbers lies between $\frac{2}{3}$ and $\frac{3}{4}$?

a. $\frac{5}{6}$
b. $\frac{9}{12}$
c. $\frac{17}{24}$
d. $\frac{12}{13}$

19. We have two right triangular prisms. Both have bases that are right triangles. The base of prism *A* has legs of lengths 3 cm and 4 cm and a hypotenuse of length 5 cm. The base of prism *B* has legs of lengths 5 cm and 12 cm and a hypotenuse of length 13 cm. If prism *A* has a height of 20 cm, what is the smallest whole-number height that prism *B* can have to make its surface area greater than that of prism *A*?

a. 3 cm
b. 7 cm
c. 8 cm
d. 10 cm

20. Examine (I), (II), and (III) and select the best answer.

(I) 0.8×0.7
(II) 0.08×0.07
(III) 0.008×0.007

a. (I) > (II) > (III)
b. (I) < (II) < (III)
c. (I) = (II) = (III)
d. (I) > (II) < (III)

21. Which number should come next in the sequence 2,011, 1,999, 1,987, 1,975, __?

a. 1,969
b. 1,968
c. 1,963
d. 1,959

22. Which of the following rules describes the sequence 5, 25, 125, 625, ...?

a. Multiply the position number by 5.
b. Raise 5 to a power equal to the position number.
c. Multiply 5 by the square of the position number.
d. Add the product of 5 and the position number to 5.

23. Tyler is one year older than 3 times Clay's age. The sum of their ages is 21. How old is Tyler?

a. 5
b. 6
c. 15
d. 16

24. We have a cube and a box (also known as a rectangular solid). The edge length of the cube is 4 feet. The box is 7 feet long, 4 feet wide, and 2 feet high. How do the volumes and surface areas of these two solids compare?

a. The cube has the larger volume, and the box has the larger surface area.
b. The box has the larger volume and the larger surface area.
c. The box has the larger volume, and the cube has the larger surface area.
d. The cube has the larger volume and the larger surface area.

25. Examine (I), (II), and (III) and select the best answer.

(I) $4 \times (7 \times 8)$
(II) $(4 \times 7) \times 8$
(III) $4 \times 7 \times 8$

a. (I) = (II) = (III)
b. (I) = (II) ≠ (III)
c. (I) ≠ (II) = (III)
d. (I) ≠ (II) ≠ (III)

26. Which of the following numbers is greatest?

a. $\frac{1}{3}$
b. $\frac{10}{33}$
c. $\frac{100}{333}$
d. $\frac{100}{330}$

27. Which number should come next in the sequence 7, 14, 28, 56, __?

a. 122
b. 112
c. 102
d. 84

28. Which of the following is the largest number?

a. $\frac{1}{2}$
b. $\frac{3}{8}$
c. $\frac{7}{16}$
d. $\frac{13}{52}$

29. We have a small cube and a large cube. The edge length of the large cube is 50% greater than that of the small cube. How do the volumes of the cubes compare?

a. The volume of the large cube is less than twice that of the small cube.
b. The volume of the large cube is between 2 and 3 times that of the small cube.
c. The volume of the large cube is between 3 and 4 times that of the small cube.
d. The volume of the large cube is more than 4 times that of the small cube.

30. If 12 is added to the product of 13 and 7, what is the result?

a. 32
b. 79
c. 103
d. 240

31. What is the 16th term in the sequence?

2, 10, 18, 26...

a. 105
b. 115
c. 122
d. 128

32. What number divided by 2 is $\frac{2}{3}$ of 66?

a. 11
b. 33
c. 44
d. 88

33. A positive integer is subtracted from a smaller positive integer. Which of the following statements is always true about the difference?

a. It is odd.
b. It is even.
c. It is positive.
d. It is negative.

34. What is the next number in the sequence?

132, 123, 115, 108, 102

a. 82
b. 87
c. 92
d. 97

35. Which number should fill in the blank in the sequence 18, 23, 27, ___, 32, 33?

a. 28
b. 29
c. 30
d. 31

36. What is the common ratio in the sequence below?

$$\frac{1}{52}, \frac{3}{52}, \frac{9}{52}, \frac{27}{52} \ldots$$

a. $\frac{1}{52}$
b. $\frac{1}{3}$
c. 3
d. 4

37. Two odd integers, one positive and one negative, are multiplied. Which of the following statements is true?

a. The product must be odd and positive.
b. The product must be even and negative.
c. The product must be odd and negative.
d. The product must be even and positive.

38. A number less than zero is multiplied by a negative number. What statement is always true about the result?

a. It is odd.
b. It is even.
c. It is positive.
d. It is negative.

39. Given the sequence $[(0,3),(1,6),(2,9),\dots,(7,y)]$, what is the value of y?

a. 12
b. 15
c. 18
d. 24

40. Which of the following must be true about the product of two even numbers?

a. It is a prime number
b. It is an odd number
c. It is a fraction
d. It is an even number

41. Examine (I), (II), and (III) and select the best answer.

(I) 90%
(II) $\frac{1}{9}$
(III) 0.9

a. (I) = (II) = (III)
b. (I) = (II) ≠ (III)
c. (I) ≠ (II) = (III)
d. (I) = (III) ≠ (II)

42. Which choice correctly shows the *n*th term formula for geometric sequences?

a. $a_n = r^{(n-1)}$
b. $a_n = a_1 r^{(n)}$
c. $a_n = a_1 r^{(n-1)}$
d. $a_n = a_1 r^{(n+1)}$

43. Examine (I), (II), and (III), and find the best answer.

(I) $(3 \times 4) + 5$
(II) $(4 + 5) \times 6$
(III) $(3 \times 5) + 6$

a. (II) < (III)
b. (I) = (II) = (III)
c. (II) = (III)
d. (I) < (II) and (II) > (III)

44. A circle has a radius of 5 feet. The perimeter of a square is longer than the circumference of this circle. If the square has an edge length that is a whole number, what is the shortest that the edge length of the square can be?

a. 5 feet
b. 7 feet
c. 8 feet
d. 20 feet

45. Circle *A* has a radius of 3 m (meters). Rectangle *B* has length 13 m and width 2 m. Square *C* has edge length 6 m. List these figures in order of their areas, from smallest to largest.

a. A, B, C
b. C, B, A
c. C, A, B
d. B, A, C

46. Which of the following statements is always true about the product of two prime numbers?

a. It is prime.
b. It is odd.
c. It is not prime.
d. It is negative.

47. An odd number is multiplied by an even number, and the result is multiplied by another odd number. Which of the following must be true about the final result?

a. It is odd
b. It is even
c. It is negative
d. It is positive

48. A cube has an edge length of 4 cm (centimeters). What is the edge length (as a whole number of centimeters) of the smallest square whose area exceeds the surface area of the cube?

a. 5 cm
b. 8 cm
c. 9 cm
d. 10 cm

49. Which number should come next in the sequence –9, –6, –3, 0, ___?

a. 9
b. 6
c. 3
d. –3

50. A ray is set up on a line as shown. If the measure of angle 1 is 90°, what can we say about the relative sizes of angle 1 and angle 2? Note: The figure is not drawn to show the relative sizes of angles correctly. Reason your answer based on the statement of the question, not on the appearance of the figure.

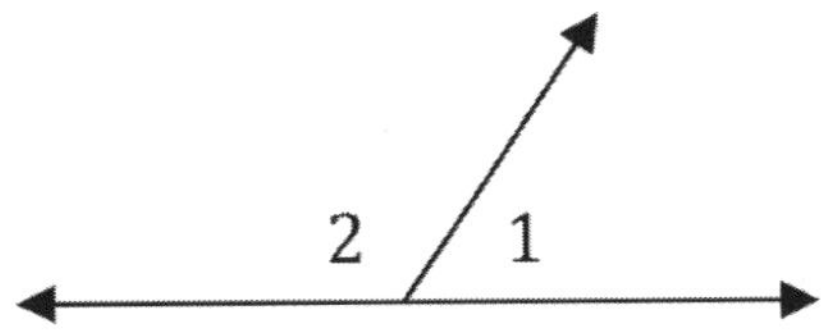

a. Angle 1 is equal to angle 2.
b. Angle 1 is larger than angle 2.
c. Angle 1 is smaller than angle 2.
d. The question does not give enough information to draw a conclusion about the relative sizes of angles 1 and 2.

51. Which number comes next in the sequence?

16, 24, 34, 46, 60

a. 56
b. 72
c. 74
d. 76

52. Which of the following values is greatest?

a. $-4 - 10$
b. $-25 - (-30)$
c. $4 \times (-20)$
d. $-2 \times (-10)$

Mathematics

1. Simplify the following expression: $4(6-3)^2 - (-2)$

a. 34
b. 38
c. 42
d. 48

2. You have just finished cooking fresh corn at 76 °C. You want to freeze it at –18 °C for long-term storage. How many degrees Celsius must you lower its temperature to be halfway to your goal temperature?

a. 29
b. 47
c. 20
d. 56

3. Rafael drives at an average speed of 36 mph on a trip that lasts 2.5 hours. How far does he travel?

a. 72 miles
b. 80 miles
c. 84 miles
d. 90 miles

4. A new candle is 21 cm high and burns at a rate of 3 cm per hour. When the candle is 9 cm high, how long has it been burning?

a. 3 hours
b. 3.5 hours
c. 4 hours
d. 4.5 hours

5. Which of the following expressions is equivalent to $(3x^{-2})^3$?

a. $9x^{-6}$
b. $9x^6$
c. $27x^{-4}$
d. $27x^{-6}$

6. Vivian has $50. She goes to the store and buys a calculator. Then she buys a book that costs half what the calculator cost. Then she buys a pen that costs half what the book cost. She has $15 left. How much did she spend on the calculator?

a. $14
b. $15
c. $18
d. $20

7. Determine the volume of a rectangular box with a length of 5 inches, a height of 7 inches, and a width of 9 inches. Round to the nearest inch.

a. 445 in^3
b. 315 in^3
c. 45 in^3
d. 35 in^3

8. Which of the following is the solution to the inequality $4x - 12 < 4$?

a. $x < 2$
b. $x > 2$
c. $x > 4$
d. $x < 4$

9. What is the value of the expression $-3 \times 5^2 + 2(4 - 18) + 33$?

a. -130
b. -70
c. -20
d. 74

10. A courier service maintains a fleet of 60 vehicles. Three-fifths of the vehicles are trucks, and the remainders are compact cars. In order to save on fuel costs, the service plans to replace half of the compact cars with hybrid vehicles. How many hybrids will they buy?

a. 24
b. 12
c. 6
d. 3

11. A man has $1,000. He adds 10% to the total amount of money. Then he takes away 10% of the new total amount. How much money does he have now?

a. $890
b. $900
c. $990
d. $1,000

12. Which of these is a net of a triangular pyramid?

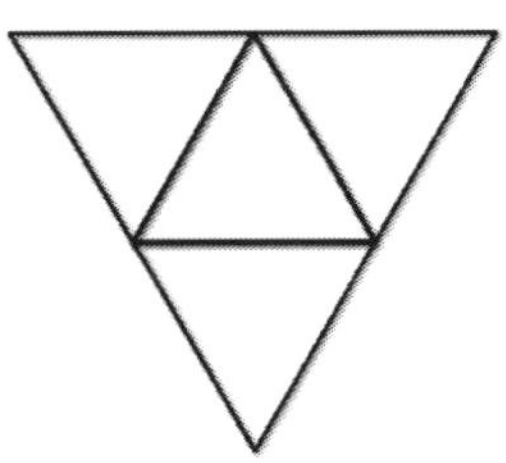
a.

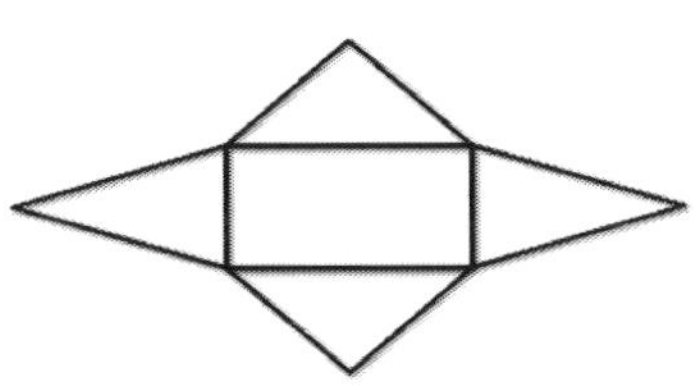
b.

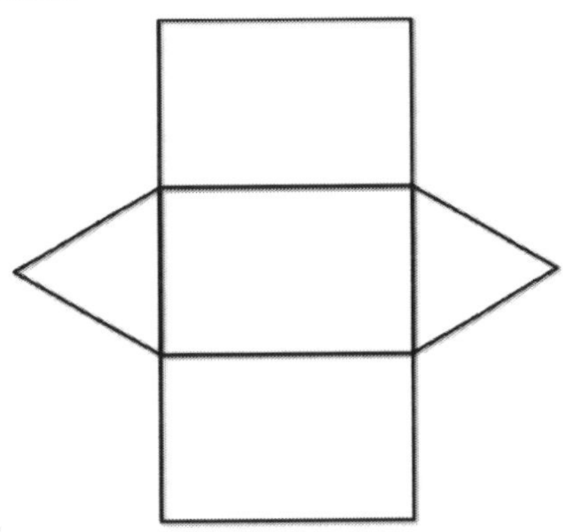
c.

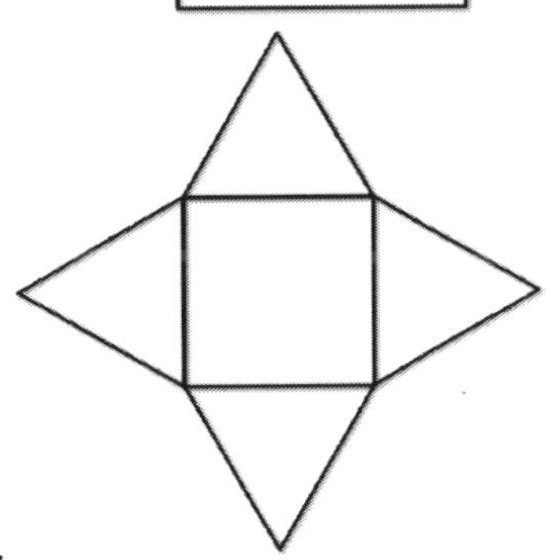
d.

13. Which of the following represents a function?

a. $\{(2,9), (3,5), (6,8), (-1,-6), (3,-2)\}$
b. $\{(8,8), (7,9), (2,1), (8,3), (3,6)\}$
c. $\{(-4,6), (2,4), (-4,-2), (3,5), (9,2)\}$
d. $\{(2,6), (6,5), (5,9), (1,0), (-3,1)\}$

14. For the number set $\{7, 12, 5, 16, 23, 44, 18, 9, Z\}$, which of the following values could be equal to Z if Z is the median of the set?

a. 11
b. 18
c. 14
d. 17

15. Three coins are tossed. What is the probability of the result being 3 heads?

a. $\frac{1}{4}$
b. $\frac{1}{6}$
c. $\frac{1}{8}$
d. $\frac{1}{16}$

16. In the figure below, line segments $\overline{AB}$ and $\overline{CD}$ are parallel and are intersected by a third line. If $\alpha = 135°$, what is the measure of δ?

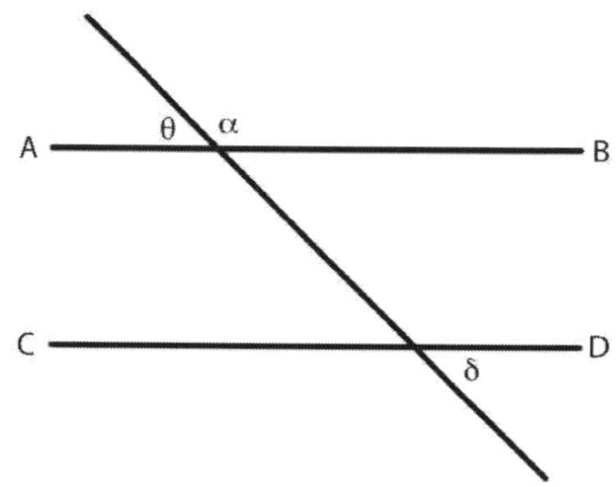

a. 135°
b. 45°
c. 35°
d. 30°

17. Kevin has 2 blue shirts, 6 black shirts, and 4 red shirts, which he keeps in the same drawer of his dresser. If he selects a shirt at random, what is the probability that it will be red or blue?

a. 25%
b. 50%
c. 60%
d. 65%

18. Tom deposits $3,800 dollars in a savings account that pays 7% interest annually. How much does he have after one year?

a. $4,110.55
b. $4,075.13
c. $4,066.00
d. $4,052.70

19. Gabriel buys a $22 book from a mail order firm. He must also pay a 10% tax and an additional $4 for shipping. What is his total cost for the book?

a. $28.20
b. $27.20
c. $26.20
d. $24.20

20. Evaluate $15 + (16 - [2(11 - 6)] - 3)$

a. 15
b. 18
c. 28
d. 30

21. Ben's current monthly rent is $750. He is moving to another apartment complex, where the monthly rent will be $900. What is the percent increase in his monthly rent amount?

a. 15%
b. 17.5%
c. 19.25%
d. 20%

22. What is $(x^2)^3 \cdot (y^2)^5 \cdot (y^4)^3$?

a. x^6y^{22}
b. x^6y^{120}
c. x^5y^{14}
d. x^6y^{-2}

23. The graph below shows the number of miles Jen runs each day, Monday through Friday. What fraction of the time does she run at least four miles?

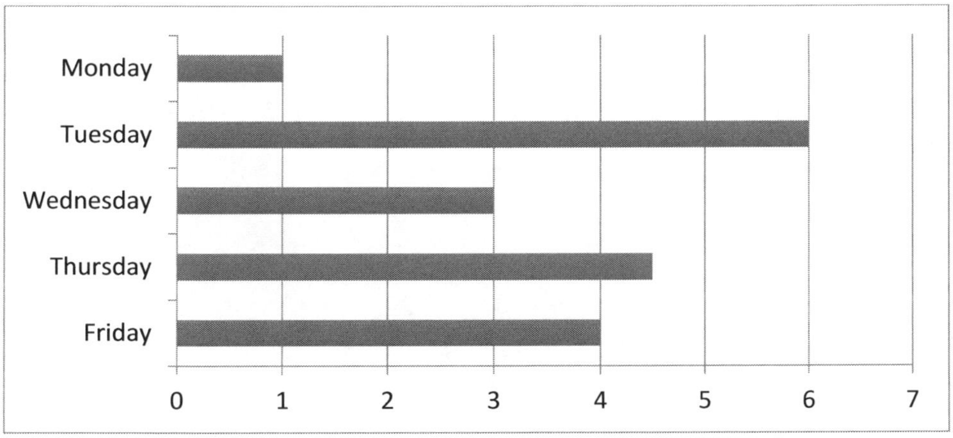

a. $\frac{3}{7}$
b. $\frac{3}{2}$
c. $\frac{2}{5}$
d. $\frac{3}{5}$

24. Simplify the following expression: $\frac{1}{4} \times \frac{3}{5} \div 1\frac{1}{8}$.

a. $\frac{8}{15}$
b. $\frac{27}{160}$
c. $\frac{2}{15}$
d. $\frac{27}{40}$

25. How many meters are equivalent to 7,200 centimeters?

a. 720,000
b. 720
c. 72
d. 7.2

26. If $a - 16 = 8b + 6$, what does $a + 3$ equal?

a. $b + 3$
b. $8b + 19$
c. $8b + 22$
d. $8b + 25$

27. Jeremy put a heavy chalk mark on the tire of his bicycle. His bike tire is 27 inches in diameter. When he rolled the bike, the chalk left marks on the sidewalk. Which expression can be used to best determine the distance, in inches, the bike rolled from the first mark to the fourth mark?

a. $3(27\pi)$
b. $4\pi(27)$
c. $(27 \div 3)\pi$
d. $(27 \div 4)\pi$

28. If a bag of balloons consists of 37 white balloons, 8 yellow balloons, and 15 black balloons, what is the probability that a balloon chosen randomly from the bag will be black?

a. 29%
b. 25%
c. 21%
d. 17%

29. At the beginning of the year 2000, 35% of the company sales were in electronics. The table below shows how electronic sales percentage has changed for the company over the years. Find the percentage of sales in electronics at the end of 2005.

Years	Difference
2000–2001	-2%
2001–2002	−1%
2002–2003	+6%
2003–2004	−1%
2004–2005	+2%

a. 2%
b. 4%
c. 39%
d. 42%

30. If $3x + 5 = 11$, then what is the value of x?

a. 6
b. 3
c. 2
d. 1

31. How many inches are in 4 feet?

a. 48
b. 36
c. 24
d. 12

32. Sandra needs $3 more to buy a $12 book. How much money does she already have?

a. $10
b. $9
c. $8
d. $7

33. The graph below shows the average temperatures for each month during the year in the city of Los Amares. During which period does the average temperature decrease by the greatest amount?

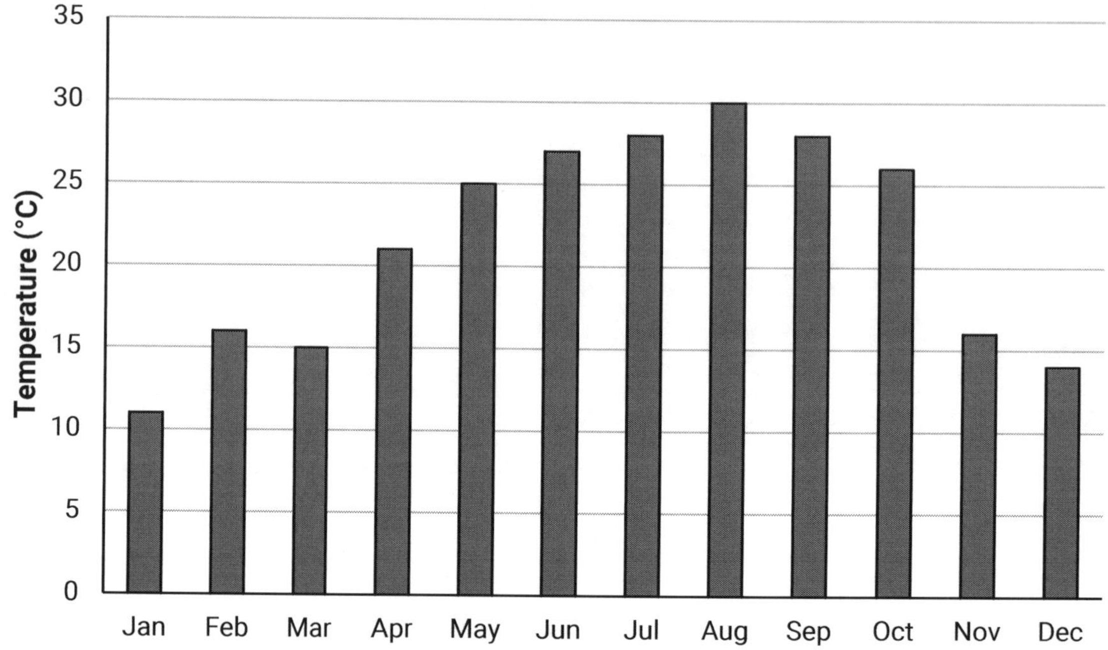

a. December to January
b. August to September
c. March to April
d. October to November

34. If it takes Alice 12 minutes to make 1 ring, how many rings can she make in 6 hours?

a. 2 rings
b. 6 rings
c. 30 rings
d. 72 rings

35. Andrea puts 10% of her paycheck into a savings account every week. At the end of a year (52 weeks), she has $1,560 in her account. Assuming no interest has been paid, what is the amount of her weekly paycheck?

a. $30
b. $120
c. $300
d. $360

36. If there are 2.54 centimeters in an inch and 36 inches in a yard, how many centimeters are in $5\frac{1}{3}$ yards?

a. 75.60 cm
b. 152.40 cm
c. 182.88 cm
d. 487.68 cm

37. Ray and his brother win a prize and share it equally. If each receives $15, what was the amount of the prize?

a. $15
b. $20
c. $30
d. $40

38. The ratio of left-handed to right-handed ballplayers on the girls' softball team is 2 : 3. If there are 12 left-handed players on the team, how many girls are on the roster in all?

a. 18
b. 24
c. 30
d. 32

39. Which frequency table is represented by the histogram shown below?

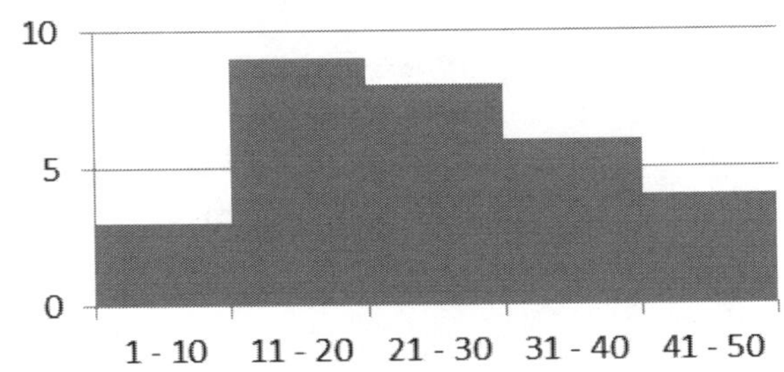

a.

Interval	Frequency
1 – 10	3
11 – 20	9
21 – 30	8
31 – 40	6
41 – 50	4

b.

Interval	Frequency
1 – 10	3
11 – 20	8
21 – 30	8
31 – 40	6
41 – 50	3

c.

Interval	Frequency
1 – 10	3
11 – 20	9
21 – 30	8
31 – 40	5
41 – 50	4

d.

Interval	Frequency
1 – 10	2
11 – 20	9
21 – 30	8
31 – 40	6
41 – 50	5

40. Which of the following represents the negative square root of 100?

a. $\sqrt{-100}$
b. $\sqrt{100}$
c. $\sqrt{10}$
d. $-\sqrt{100}$

41. Two hikers start at a ranger station and leave at the same time. One hiker heads due west at 3 mph. The other hiker heads due north at 4 mph. How far apart are the hikers after 2 hours of hiking?

a. 5 miles
b. 7 miles
c. 10 miles
d. 14 miles

42. How many prime factors does the number 93 have?

a. 2
b. 3
c. 4
d. 5

43. What is the area of a square with a perimeter of 44 cm?

a. 11 cm^2
b. 16 cm^2
c. 121 cm^2
d. 1,936 cm^2

Refer to the following for question 44:

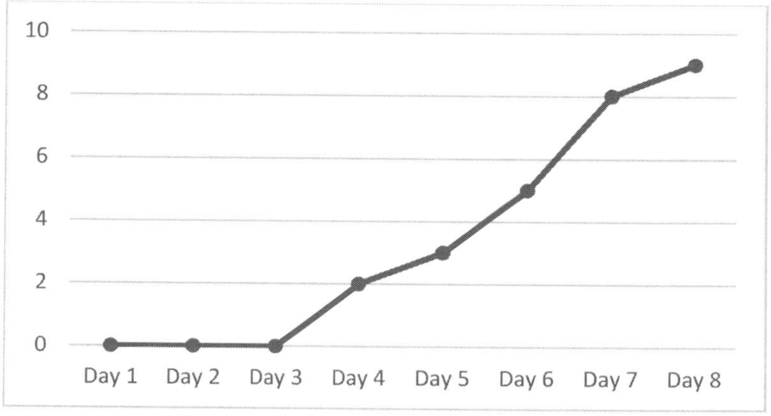

Beth plants a number of sunflower seeds and checks daily to see if any have sprouted. The graph above shows how many seedlings are growing each day when she checks.

44. Which day did the first seedling appear?

a. Day 1
b. Day 2
c. Day 3
d. Day 4

45. If one side of a square has a length of 56 cm, what is its perimeter?

a. 112 cm
b. 224 cm
c. 448 cm
d. 3,136 cm

46. Which of the following represents a function?

a. $\{(2,1),(3,-2),(6,8),(-1,-4),(4,-1)\}$
b. $\{(8,5),(7,9),(3,1),(4,7),(3,6)\}$
c. $\{(-4,6),(2,3),(4,-2),(3,6),(-4,2)\}$
d. $\{(2,6),(6,1),(5,8),(2,-1),(-3,1)\}$

47. There are 12 inches in a foot. Which of the following is equivalent to 3 feet 4 inches?

a. $3\frac{1}{2}$ feet
b. $3\frac{1}{6}$ feet
c. $3\frac{3}{4}$ feet
d. $3\frac{1}{3}$ feet

48. A crane raises one end of a 3,300-pound steel beam. The other end rests upon the ground. If the crane supports 30% of the beam's weight, how many pounds does it support?

a. 330 lb
b. 700 lb
c. 990 lb
d. 1,100 lb

49. Simplify the expression: $5(80 \div 8) + (7 - 2) - (9 \times 5)$

a. -150
b. 10
c. 100
d. 230

50. Convert 14.75 kilograms to decigrams.

a. 147,500 dg
b. 14,750 dg
c. 1.475 dg
d. 0.1475 dg

51. In the figure below, line segment $\overline{AC}$ bisects $\angle BAD$. If the measure of $\angle BAC$ is 15°, what is the measure of $\angle BAD$?

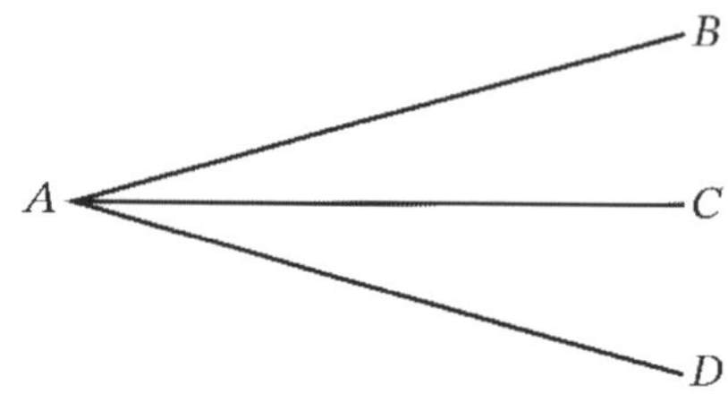

a. 45°
b. 30°
c. 20°
d. 15°

52. A teacher asked her students how many hours of television they watched over the weekend. The results are displayed below. How many students watched more than 8 hours of television over the weekend?

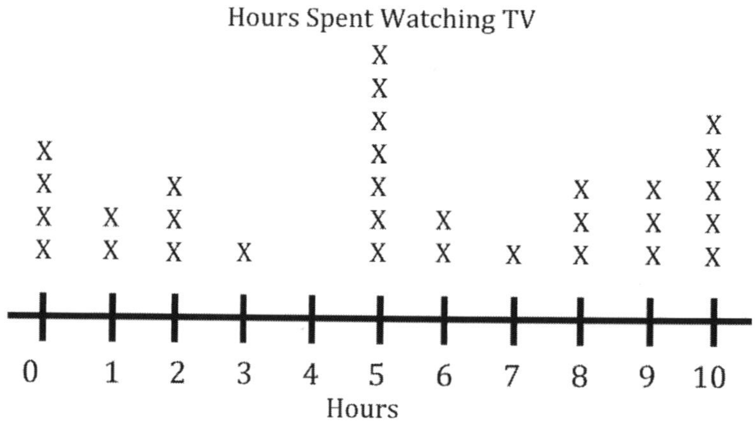

a. 3 students
b. 8 students
c. 11 students
d. 20 students

53. In the figure below, lines a and b are parallel. Find the value of x.

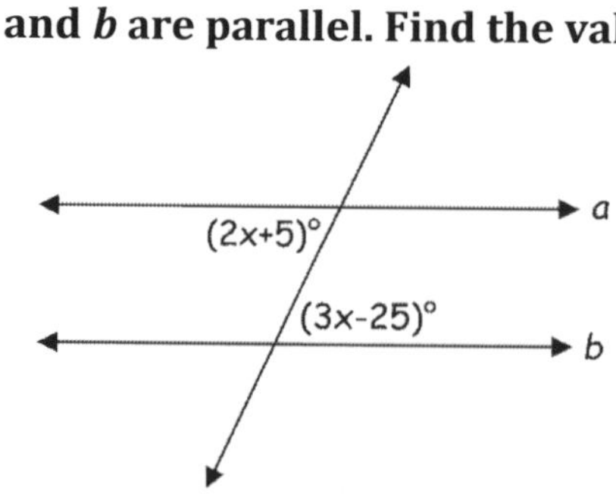

a. $x = 22$
b. $x = 30$
c. $x = 40$
d. $x = 55$

54. What is the value of the expression $2(7+8)^2 - 12\ (6 \times 2)$?

a. 119
b. 225
c. 306
d. 604

55. Quentin buys a computer game that has been marked down by $25. He pays 80% of the normal price. What was the normal price of the computer game, before the mark down?

a. $75
b. $100
c. $125
d. $160

56. Which of the following numbers is a prime factor of the number 121?

a. 13
b. 12
c. 11
d. 8

57. If 120 customers purchased coffee today, and this is $\frac{1}{4}$ less than yesterday, how many people purchased coffee yesterday?

a. 90
b. 150
c. 160
d. 240

58. Brain tumors are diagnosed at a rate of 12 per 100,000 people per year. Cell phone users have been shown to be 240% as likely to have a brain tumor as others. How many brain tumors per 100,000 cell phone users are expected annually?

a. 240
b. 30.6
c. 28.8
d. 24.4

59. Simplify the expression $(10 + 4 \times 3) \div 2$.

a. 22
b. 21
c. 6
d. 11

60. The radius of a circle with an area of 31 square units is doubled. What is the area of the new circle?

a. 62 square units
b. 93 square units
c. 124 square units
d. 132 square units

61. What is the greatest integer value of y for which $5y - 20 < 0$?

a. 5
b. 4
c. 3
d. 2

Refer to the following for question 62:

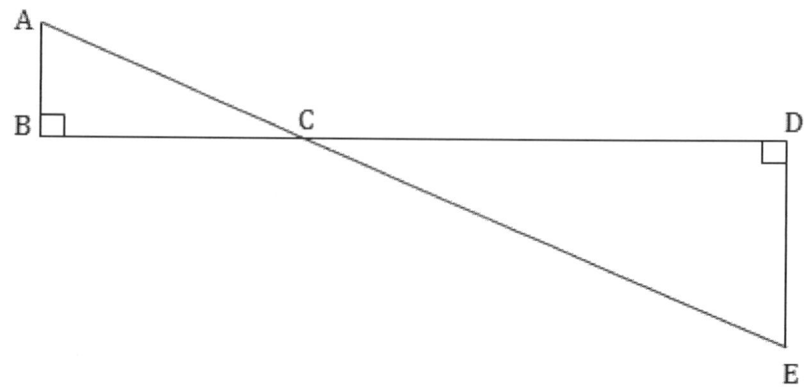

62. In the figure above, $\overline{BC}$ is 4 units long. Segment $\overline{CD}$ is 8 units long. Segment $\overline{DE}$ is 6 units long. What is the length of segment $\overline{AC}$?

a. 7 units
b. 5 units
c. 3 units
d. 2.5 units

63. How many pounds are equivalent to 32 ounces?

a. 16
b. 8
c. 4
d. 2

64. Which of the following choices best describes a three-dimensional figure comprised of only one square base and four triangular sides?

a. Square prism
b. Triangular prism
c. Triangular pyramid
d. Square pyramid

Answer Key and Explanations for Test #1

Reading—Comprehension

1. A: Since the passage does not promote one view over the other, Answers B and C are incorrect. Whereas the passage does criticize both methods, it also explores their strengths, so Answer D is incorrect. Answer A is the best choice.

2. C: This term should be easy enough to define based on knowledge of the prefix and root; if not, scanning the text will reveal the answer. Answer B may be a deceptive choice since co-sleeping is associated with attachment parenting, but Answer C is the strongest response.

3. C: The final sentence of the last paragraph reads, "In the end, parents must rely on the only tried and true technique: trial and error." Only Answer C is consistent with this statement. Answer A is not addressed in the passage, and Answers B and C are at odds with the final sentence.

4. A: Answer A is the only answer with any connection to Ferber's "cry it out" method. Answer B is closer to the "attachment parenting" method. Answers C and D are not mentioned in the text.

5. C: While the term "contradictory" implies something that might be false (Answer A), deceitful (Answer B), or even inexact (Answer D), the meaning in the sentence is closest to Answer C, conflicting.

6. B: Answer A is incorrect because it is closer to Dr. Ferber's "cry it out" method. Answers C and D are not mentioned in the text. Answer B is the best answer.

7. B: In the sentence, the word "callous" is paired with the word "uncaring," the closest synonym of which is Answer B. Answers A and C are antonyms of "callous." Answer D is loosely connected to the discussion, but it is not a close synonym of "callous."

8. D: Answer D is implied in the last sentence, which suggests that parents use trial and error to figure out what works for them. Answers A and B are not directly addressed in the passage; Answer C may be implied, but it is not the main idea.

9. B: This question asks about the purpose of the passage. Just scanning the first word of each answer can help determine the best choice. This passage attempts to explain, not persuade or argue. Whereas answer D sounds somewhat true, the passage does not so much teach the process as give a brief overview. Answer B is the best choice.

10. A: Answer A is closest to the meaning of the word as used in the sentence. Whereas Answers B and D may both be related to the term, they are not adequate substitutes for it. Answer C is related to the discussion in paragraph 3, but not to this particular word.

11. D: Answer D is the only statement whose truth can be established by reading the passage. Answer A is not addressed in the passage. Answers B and C contain extreme, all-inclusive words like "all" and "only," which are red flags for an untrue statement.

12. C: Only Answer C is justified by the last paragraph. Answer A seems related to the paragraph, but it exaggerates. Answer B and D are not stated anywhere in the paragraph or the passage.

13. C: The meaning of the term "reverb" can be found in the sentence that reads, "The mixer will choose [...] whether to add certain textures to the sound, such as reverb or echo, which both make some instruments sound further away than others." Answers A and B are somewhat deceptive because they sound like they might be related to the term. The word starts with the prefix "re-," which generally means to repeat something, so answer A is appealing. Answer B starts with the same prefix and is also tempting. Both are incorrect, though, as a quick scan of the sentence in the passage will reveal. Answer D is inconsistent with the passage.

14. A: Answer A is the only statement that can be logically deduced from the paragraph. Answers B, C, and D are not stated in the passage. Answer D may seem momentarily tempting because it sounds like it can be logically inferred from the paragraph, but a closer reading will discredit this answer; so will the fact that it is far from true.

15. A: Again, the answer can be found by scanning the sentence that contains the word. The sentence reads, "Samples, short recorded sounds triggered by a computer or keyboard."

16. D: This question will likely require you to read each answer carefully. It asks you to remember specific information from each of the paragraphs. Answer D is confirmed by the first sentence in paragraph 2, "Recording involves using microphones." None of the other statements can be confirmed by reading the passage.

17. B: In the sentence, "If you've ever seen the white condensation that rises above a pot of boiling water, then you've seen a cloud up close," the word "steam" could easily replace the word condensation. Answers A and D are incompatible with the sentence. Answer C, though related in meaning, is not as appropriate as Answer B, steam.

18. A: Answer A is the only sentence that is fully supported by the passage. Answers B, C, and D are not discussed in the passage.

19. C: This answer can be deduced from the sentence containing the word "currents." The sentence reads, "The currents of air in the atmosphere hold these tiny droplets up." Answers A and B, though they are both associated with the word "currents," are not mentioned anywhere in the passage. Answer D, "Vapor," though relevant to the discussion, is not mentioned as something that can hold up tiny droplets of water.

20. C: Answer C is the only answer that captures the main idea of the passage as a whole. The other answers reflect various ideas implied within specific paragraphs but not the overall passage.

21. A: This question addresses how the passage is written. Answer A is correct because the three questions provide a brief preview of the rest of the passage, in effect giving an overview of the passage's organization. Answer B is incorrect and answers C and D are easy to eliminate because they use words like "all" and "always."

22. D: Answer D is the only statement that can be correctly inferred from the paragraph. Answer A contradicts the paragraph; B and C are not mentioned in the paragraph.

23. B: Answer B is the only answer that is consistent with the information presented in the passage. The fourth paragraph reads, "When sunlight [...] passes through the tiny droplets in a cloud, it scatters all the different colors of light in every direction." Answers A, C, and D are not addressed in the passage.

24. B: Paragraph 2 states, "This vapor is invisible until it reaches higher levels of the atmosphere, where the temperature is much colder. There the water vapor begins to cool down and turn back into tiny droplets of water." Answer B is the only answer that fits with this explanation. Answer A may sound true, but it is not mentioned in the passage. Answers C and D are inconsistent with the passage, not to mention untrue.

25. A: Answer A is the best answer because the question asks for the main topic. Each of the other answers addresses the specific examples used in the paragraph, not the main topic.

26. B: The sentence in which the word is found reads, "There [in Persia] he allied himself with a local governor, or satrap." A quick scan of this sentence and the one preceding it should help eliminate all the other answers.

27. C: While any of these answers could account for Alcibiades' murder, only Answer C is accurate. Since the final paragraph mentions two accounts of Alcibiades' death, the best inference is that we don't know which one is true.

28. A: Only answer A is consistent with the meaning of the sentence the word is found in. Answers B and C are both related to the passage, but not the word. Answer D is far-fetched.

29. C: The use of the phrase "by coincidence" in the first sentence of the third paragraph helps us rule out answers A and D. No mention is made of the satrap in relation to Alcibiades' castle, so we can rule out Answer B. The process of elimination, as well as a quick scan of the end of paragraph three and the beginning of paragraph four, leaves us with choice C.

30. A: Like many other questions about the purpose of a passage, a quick glance at the first word of each answer can help eliminate incorrect answers. The passage is not written to persuade, which rules out Answer B; nor does it put forth much argumentation or reasoning, which rules out Answers C and D.

31. D: An ally is a confidant, so Answer D is the best choice. Answer A can be eliminated because the passage makes no mention of spying on the satrap. Answers C and D are tempting because they are related to the passage, but neither answer is in keeping with the meaning of the word "ally."

32. B: Answer B is the only answer that is broad enough to apply to the passage as a whole. Answers A and D are too narrow. Answer C may be broad enough, but nowhere in the passage does it mention Alcibiades' desire to become king.

33. C: Whereas in paragraph three this passage does touch on the debatable interpretations of quantum weirdness; the passage is not overtly trying to prove a point. Instead it is attempting to inform the reader of the unusual properties of the subatomic realm. Answer C is the best choice.

34. A: Answer A is the correct answer, though Answers B and D may be tempting because of the shared roots among "physics," "physiology," and "physical education." Answer C is a red herring; while it is true that some physicists study subatomic particles, the best choice is still Answer A.

35. A: In the passage, the number is followed by the statement, "This is a very small number," which is the equivalent of "a minuscule number," Answer A. Answers C and D are not mentioned anywhere in the passage.

36. B: Answers A and C are easy to eliminate because of the extreme wording. Answer D is unfounded based on the passage. Answer B is the best answer based on paragraph 3.

37. C: Answer C is easy to derive from the prefix and root of the word subatomic. Answers A and D can be eliminated because no mention of molecules is made in the passage. Answer B is related to the discussion in paragraph 3, but is incorrect.

38. C: Scanning the sentence containing the word should reveal the answer. Answers A and D are far-fetched; Answer B is deceptive, but again there is no mention of molecules in the passage.

39. A: Scanning the first word of each answer does not help with the process of elimination because each one starts with "some." Answer A best captures the sentence's meaning. Answers B and C are inconsistent with the meaning of the paragraph; Answer D sounds far-fetched and should be easy to eliminate.

40. C: Answer A is unlikely because of its all-inclusive wording. Answer B contradicts the final sentence of the passage. Answer D is inconsistent with the passage as a whole. Answer C is the most plausible answer.

Reading—Vocabulary

1. D: Slight can mean insult when used as a noun.

2. B: Mortified means embarrassed.

3. A: A perimeter is a boundary.

4. C: Slumber is another word for sleep. Saying someone slumbered is the same as saying they slept.

5. C: To say something was done instantly means that it was done immediately and without hesitation.

6. A: Persistent most nearly means ongoing.

7. A: Disadvantaged most nearly means deprived.

8. A: To have doubts is to have uncertainties or hesitations. To say that someone is doubtful about something means that they are uncertain.

9. A: To recuperate is to heal.

10. D: When something is described as tidy, it usually means that it is neat and that things are in their proper place. Saying a house is tidy and saying it is neat conveys the same meaning.

11. D: Somebody who is experiencing or feeling anguish is experiencing sorrow or sadness.

12. A: Faltering means hesitating or wavering.

13. D: Volatile means explosive.

14. A: Shrill suggests something high-pitched.

15. D: A hypocritical person is someone whose actions contradict the values they hold others to. Insincere is the closest synonym in this list.

16. B: Vital most nearly has the same meaning as essential.

17. D: When something is concluded, it means that it is finished or completed.

18. D: Migrate most nearly has the same meaning as relocate.

19. B: Formidable most nearly has the same meaning as intimidating.

20. D: Coherent most nearly has the same meaning as logical.

21. A: Describing something as accurate and describing it as correct conveys the same meaning. For example, saying somebody accurately predicted something is the same as saying they correctly predicted something.

22. D: The word difficulty implies hardship. When it is said that somebody is having difficulties with another person or thing, it usually means they are experiencing problems.

Language

1. B: Comma. The comma in front of the phrase "the German shepherd" sets it off, and it must be followed by a comma as well.

2. D: None of these sentences contains a mistake.

3. A: Fragment. Though this sentence contains a subject, "population," it contains no predicate.

4. C: Pronoun-antecedent agreement. The pronoun "his" does not agree with its antecedent, "farmers."

5. B: Comma splice. There are really two sentences here, one before and one after the comma. Two complete sentences joined together with a comma is a comma splice. Sentence A contains an apostrophe that might throw some readers for a moment, but closer reading will show that the word neighbors can be plural in this sentence, so the apostrophe is in the correct position.

6. D: None of these sentences contains a mistake.

7. C: Subject-verb disagreement. Despite the word "there" at the beginning, "vegetables" is the real subject of this sentence. When the words "there is" or "there are" come at the beginning of a sentence, the verb ("is" or "are") should always agree with the subject of the sentence. In this case, the subject is "vegetables," and the verb should be "are" because "vegetables" is plural.

8. C: Subject-verb disagreement. The verb of this sentence is "remembers," and the subject is "Students." When there is a long clause in between the subject and the verb of a sentence, it's easy to miss the subject-verb disagreement.

9. C: Adverb/Adjective. The adverb "separately" should be written as the adjective "separate."

10. B: Fused sentence. Sentence B is known as a fused sentence or a run-on. It contains two sentences jammed together with no punctuation.

11. D: None of these sentences contains a mistake.

12. D: None of these sentences contains a mistake.

13. C: Subject-verb disagreement. The pronoun "no one" is always singular. Here the verb "were" is plural and does not agree with "no one."

14. A: Verb tense. The verb in the first clause of the sentence is in the past tense, but the verb at the end is in present. "Get" should read "got."

15. A: Subject-verb disagreement. "Kills" is a singular verb, but it does not agree with the plural "fishermen," which is the subject of the sentence.

16. A: Comma splice. Sentence A is a comma splice because it fuses two complete sentences together with a comma.

17. B: Apostrophe. The apostrophe on the word "Congress'" does not need to be there.

18. B: Double negative. The phrase "couldn't hardly" is nonstandard because it forms a double negative.

19. C: Fragment. Sentence C is a dependent clause, which cannot stand on its own.

20. B: Subject-verb disagreement. The subject of the sentence is a compound plural, "night and day," and it requires a plural verb. The sentence should read, "night and day are the same length."

21. C: Comma splice. These two sentences are fused together with a comma, making this sentence a comma splice.

22. B: Subject-verb disagreement. The plural verb "mow" does not agree with the singular subject, "Pete."

23. C: Punctuation. Though the sentence talks about a question, the sentence is itself declarative and requires a period.

24. A: Capitalization. The word "People" does not need to be capitalized.

25. C: Comma. There should be a comma to separate the digits in the date at the end of this sentence.

26. A: Capitalization. "African" should be capitalized.

27. A: Subject-verb disagreement. The compound subject is "Belgium, The Netherlands, and Luxembourg" and requires a plural verb. The singular verb "is" does not agree with the plural subject.

28. D: None of these sentences contains a mistake.

29. C: Fused sentence. This sentence is a run-on or a fused sentence. It joins two complete sentences without any punctuation.

30. C: Verb. Since "to write" is in the infinitive form, the verb should not take an ending. "To writes" is incorrect.

31. D: All of the sentences are correct.

32. A: Capitalization. The word "house" does not need to be capitalized.

33. B: Apostrophe. The contraction "couldn't" requires an apostrophe between the "n" and the "t."

34. A: Verb. "Hitted" is incorrect verb usage.

35. D: None of these sentences contains a mistake.

36. C: Comma. The list of words at the end of this sentence needs commas to separate each item.

37. D: None of these sentences contains a mistake.

38. B: Comma. There is no need to place a comma in the middle of this sentence.

39. A: Capitalization. The word "soprano" does not need to be capitalized.

40. B: Comma. The list in the middle of this sentence requires commas after the words "toothpaste" and "toothbrush."

41. D: None of these sentences contains a mistake.

42. C: Verb. "Mights" is not a correct verb form.

43. B: The word "then" is incorrect in this context. It should be "than."

44. A: The word "garrage" should be spelled "garage."

45. D: None of the sentences contains a spelling mistake.

46. B: "Soul" should be spelled "sole."

47. D: None of these sentences contains a spelling mistake.

48. A: "Loosing" should be spelled "losing."

49. C: "Neice" should be spelled "niece."

50. B: "Evenning" only has one "n" and should read "evening."

51. B: The sentence fits best after sentence 2 because it explicitly refers back to the terms used in sentence 2. The phrase "problematic beliefs" shows up in both sentences.

52. D: The sentence fits best after sentence 4 because it contains a statement that directly contrasts with the statement made in sentence 4.

53. A: Since the second part of the clause contrasts with the first part, the conjunction "but" is the best choice.

54. B: All of the choices except for "because" indicate contrast, but these two clauses do not contrast with each other.

55. A: Since the two clauses contrast with each other, "but" is the best choice.

56. C: All of the sentences except for sentence C are confusingly worded and written in the passive voice.

57. B: All of the sentences except B are poorly worded or they contain verb errors.

58. A: All of the sentences except A are poorly worded or they contain verb errors.

59. C: Sentence 4 is only tangentially related to the discussion of recycling rubber tires.

60. A: The sentence about Bob Dylan's best records is not directly relevant to the discussion, nor is it consistent with the tone of the discussion.

Verbal Skills

1. A: Cordial means warm and friendly, the opposite of inhospitable.

2. A: Furniture is the general class that all the other words in this group fit into.

3. A: Mutiny most nearly means revolt.

4. C: "Appliance" is a general category that the other words in the list belong to. Toasters, ovens, and coffee makers are all appliances.

5. D: Fragrant, ambrosial, and aromatic all describe a good or desirable scent. Conversely, malodorous describes an unpleasant odor or smell.

6. B: The first two sentences can be diagrammed as follows: Reece > Lee > Darren. Sentence three, Darren > Reece, is inconsistent with the first two sentences. It is false.

7. B: An apple develops from a seed; a person develops from an embryo.

8. C: Escalate means rise, which is the opposite of plummet.

9. D: Potent means powerful or strong, while weak means frail or feeble.

10. C: Subjective means based on feelings and opinions rather than evidence and facts, while objective means based on facts instead of personal opinions or views.

11. C: Cumulous, cirrus, and stratus are all types of clouds.

12. D: Electricity comes out of an outlet; water comes out of a faucet.

13. B: Punctuation is the general class to which the other items in the list belong.

14. D: Agitate means to trouble or make nervous, and disturb means to bother or interfere. Therefore, disturb is the best choice.

15. B: Flounder most nearly means struggle.

16. D: To attest is to vouch for or to certify.

17. A: Tasteful means refined, the opposite of vulgar.

18. C: Complete means finish, which is the opposite of begin.

19. B: We can diagram the first two statements as follows: Gianna>Javier>Caiden. The third statement says that Gianna<Caiden, which is inconsistent with the first two statements, so it is false.

20. A: To commence something is to begin or start something.

21. A: Optimum most nearly means ideal.

22. A: Candor means open or forthright, and honesty means an adherence to the truth or facts. Therefore, honesty would be the best choice.

23. B: The first two sentences can be diagrammed as follows: Esther=Marcus; Lee > Marcus. If Lee drove farther than Marcus, he also drove farther than Esther. The third sentence, which we can diagram as Esther > Lee, contradicts sentences one and two, so it is false.

24. B: Annoying means causing irritation, which is the opposite of pleasing.

25. A: Abrasive means to be harsh or demonstrate a lack of concern for others, and irritating means to serve as an annoyance or bother. Therefore, irritating is the best choice.

26. D: Marry most nearly means join.

27. A: A pledge is a promise, the opposite of breach, which is the violation or breaking of a promise.

28. D: Furniture is the category to which the other answers belong.

29. B: Shun means reject or ignore, the opposite of embrace.

30. B: Liable most nearly means responsible.

31. A: The words inflammable, ignitable, and combustible all describe choice A, gasoline.

32. C: The other answers are all types of dogs, while a cardinal is a type of bird.

33. B: False

The first two sentences can be diagrammed as follows: Soccer>football>baseball. Sentence three, baseball>soccer, is inconsistent with the first two sentences. It is false.

34. A: Mindful means thoughtful, the opposite of inattentive.

35. C: An *intermission* is a pause between acts of a play. Two common types of plays are *dramas* and comedies. So, we can determine that an *intermission* is a piece to the whole of a *drama*. Now, the comparison begins with *plant* as in vegetation. So, the best answer choice is *habitat* (i.e., the place where animal and plant life are naturally living) which fills the role of being the whole to the piece of *plant*.

36. A: Temperature is used to measure heat; pounds are used to measure weight.

37. C: When reviewing the answer, keep in mind the following: greater than (>) will mean left after, and less than (<) will mean left before. We can diagram the first two statements as follows: Brett>Dane and Dane<John. The third statement can be diagrammed as John<Brett. We do not have enough information to prove that John left before Brett.

38. D: One may move across ice by skating as one may move through water by swimming. (C) does not involve mobility.

39. D: Exercise causes fitness as study causes knowledge. The other answers do not represent this causal relationship.

40. B: Cognizant means having an understanding of one's surroundings, and aware means to possess knowledge of a situation. Therefore, aware is the best choice.

41. C: Opaque most nearly means dark.

42. A: Solitary can mean a number of different things, but one meaning is single. For example, if you said there was a solitary tree in a yard, you would mean that there was a single tree.

43. A: We can diagram the first two sentences as follows: Otis > Steve=Carrie. The third sentence claims that Otis > Carrie, which is consistent with the first two sentences.

44. B: We can diagram the first two sentences as follows: The Gang Mentality > Metal Leather > The Animal Instincts. The third sentence, Gang Mentality < Metal Leather, is inconsistent with the first two.

45. B: Almost means approximately, which is the opposite of exactly.

46. C: We can diagram this account as follows: H<D, A<D. The relationship between Heather and Alice is not specified, so the third statement is uncertain.

47. A: True

The first two sentences can be diagrammed as follows: Rocco>Ashley>Brian. Sentence three, Rocco>Brian, is consistent with the first two sentences. It is true.

48. A: Obstruct, block, and barricade are all synonyms meaning to stop or slow down. Conversely, facilitate means to make easier.

49. D: *Espionage* is the service of spying on opposition in order to gain intelligence. So, the nature (or characteristic) of this task is easily understood to be *discreet* (i.e., tactful and cautious). The analogy continues with *kindling* which are the pieces of material used to start a fire. In many situations, a fire is characteristic of something tragic that is about to happen to someone or something. A name for this foreboding sense of tragedy can be *ominous*. In short, a characteristic of *kindling* is *ominous*.

50. B: Private, corporal, and sergeant are all ranks in the military. While there are military doctors and combat medics, a doctor is not specifically a military rank.

51. A: Pantomime most nearly means mimic.

52. B: Crying is an expression of sadness as yelling is an expression of anger. (C) contains this relationship but in the wrong order.

53. B: False

The first two sentences can be diagrammed as follows: Monica>Ray>Juliet. Sentence three, Juliet>Monica, is inconsistent with the first two sentences. It is false.

54. D: General means the opposite of particular.

55. B: Professional is the general category to which the other items in the list belong.

56. A: To depress is the opposite of enliven, which means to excite or invigorate.

57. C: Robust means healthy and vigorous, the opposite of sickly.

58. A: Expend means to use up or spend, while conserve means to save or protect from use.

59. B: Delaware, Hawaii, and California are all states within the United States of America. Conversely, Puerto Rico is not a US state but an unincorporated territory. Although residents are considered American citizens, they cannot vote for the president and do not have a voting representative in Congress. Also, most residents do not have to pay federal income taxes.

60. B: School is the general class to which the other items belong.

Quantitative Skills

1. B: Left triangle: $3 \times 2 = 6$ and $6 - 1 = 5$, so the middle value is 5.

Middle triangle: $5 \times 2 = 10$ and $10 - 4 = 6$, so the middle value is 6.

Right triangle: $3 \times 5 = 15$ and $15 - 7 = 8$, so the middle value will be 8.

2. B: The only integer between 4 and 6 is 5, so (I) must equal 5. Half of 10 is 5, so (II) must equal 5. The only prime number between 3 and 7 is 5, so (III) must equal 5. Since all 3 items equal 5, the statement "(I) must be equal to both (II) and (III)" is correct.

3. A: To find the distance between points, we find the difference of their coordinates (locations). The distance from point A to point B is $5 - (-3) = 8$, and the distance from point B to point C is $21 - 5 = 16$. Since 16 is twice 8, we see that point B is twice as far from point C as from point A. This means point B is not halfway between points A and C. Further, the distance from point A to point C is $21 - (-3) = 24$. Since $24 \neq 3 \times 16$, point C is not 3 times as far from point A as from point B. And since $24 < 5 \times 8$, point A is not more than 5 times as far from point C as from point B.

4. B: The values of each expression are as follows:

$$4^3 = 4 \times 4 \times 4 = 64$$
$$5^2 = 5 \times 5 = 25$$
$$3^4 = 3 \times 3 \times 3 \times 3 = 81$$

Since $64 > 25 < 81$, the expression (I) > (II) < (III) is true.

5. A: Only dividing by 5 has no remainder: $250 \div 5 = 50$. All of the other divisors leave a remainder, as follows:

$$250 \div 15 = 16 \text{ R } 10$$
$$250 \div 20 = 12 \text{ R } 10$$
$$250 \div 30 = 8 \text{ R } 10$$

Therefore, the correct answer is 5.

6. C: The sequence is geometric. Use the nth term formula for geometric sequences: $a_n = ar^{(n-1)}$.

Each term is multiplied by –2 to generate the next term of the sequence.

$$r = -2$$

The first term in the sequence is 113.

$$a = 113$$

The 6th term of the sequence is unknown.

$$n = 6$$

Substitute these values into the formula.

$$a_6 = 113(-2)^{(6-1)}$$
$$a_6 = 113(-2)^5$$
$$a_6 = 113(-32)$$
$$a_6 = -3{,}616$$

The 6th term of the sequence is -3,616.

7. C: Find the common denominator of $\frac{3}{8}$ and $\frac{13}{24}$.

$$\frac{3}{8} \times \frac{3}{3} = \frac{9}{24}$$
$$\frac{13}{24} \times \frac{1}{1} = \frac{13}{24}$$

The value must be greater than $\frac{9}{24}$ and less than $\frac{13}{24}$. The fraction $\frac{5}{12}$, when expressed as the equivalent fraction $\frac{10}{24}$, is between these two values.

8. B: Sequences are considered arithmetic when the same value is added or subtracted each time. This sequence decreases by 2 from one term to the next, therefore, it is arithmetic.

9. B: To find the unknown number, set up an equation where the value of the unknown number is n.

$$\frac{1}{2}n = 15\% \times 70$$

Solve for the value of n by first simplifying on the right side of the equation.

$$\frac{1}{2}n = 0.15 \times 70$$
$$\frac{1}{2}n = 10.5$$

Then, multiply both sides of the equation by 2.

$$n = 21$$

Therefore, the value of the unknown number is 21.

10. D: By the Pythagorean theorem, if the legs of a right triangle have lengths a and b, and the hypotenuse has length c, then $c^2 = a^2 + b^2$. In the given triangle we have $a = 5$ inches and $b =$ 6 inches, so we have $c^2 = 5^2 + 6^2 = 25 + 36 = 61$. Taking square roots gives us $c = \sqrt{61}$, which is between 7 and 8 inches (since 61 is between $7^2 = 49$ and $8^2 = 64$). Thus, the perimeter is between $5 + 6 + 7 = 18$ inches and $5 + 6 + 8 = 19$ inches.

11. C: If we call the diameter of the large circle d, then we have $C_1 = \pi d$. The diameter of each small circle is half that of the large circle, so each small circle has circumference $\pi\left(\frac{d}{2}\right)$. Thus, the sum of the circumferences of the two small circles is $C_2 = 2 \times \pi\left(\frac{d}{2}\right) = \pi d$. So, we see that C_1 and C_2 are equal, both being πd.

12. D: Each term in the sequence is generated by multiplying the previous term by –2.

$$-5 \times (-2) = 10$$
$$10 \times (-2) = -20$$
$$-20 \times (-2) = 40$$
$$40 \times (-2) = -80$$
$$-80 \times (-2) = 160$$

The next term in the sequence is 160.

13. C: The sequence represents increasing powers of 3: $3^1, 3^2, 3^3$, etc. Since $81 = 3^4$, the next element in the sequence will be 3^5, which is 243. Expressed differently, each number in the series is triple the preceding number, and $81 \times 3 = 243$.

14. C: Evaluate each of the expressions.

$$\frac{4}{5} \times 80 = 64$$
$$20\% \times 20 = 0.2 \times 20 = 4$$
$$7\% \times 1{,}400 = 0.07 \times 1{,}400 = 98$$
$$3^{(6-2)} = 3^4 = 81$$

The value 98 is largest, so the expression "7% of 1,400" is greatest.

15. C: The subtraction of a negative number is equivalent to the addition of its positive conjugate, so that $-4 - (-10)$ is the same as $-4 + 10 = 6$. The value of the other choices are as follows:

$$6 - 2 = 4$$
$$-4 - 2 = -6$$
$$11 - 6 = 5$$

Of the values 6, 4, –6, and 5, 6 is the greatest. Therefore, the expression $-4 - (-10)$ is the greatest.

16. B: If all primates are mammals, and all lemurs are primates, then all lemurs are mammals. All primates are not lemurs. Since neither whales nor monkeys are mentioned in the premises, they cannot be included in the conclusion. The conclusion can only be based on the information given in the premises. Therefore, the correct answer is choice B.

17. C: To determine this number, write an equation using the variable n to represent the unknown number.

$$8n = 5 + 59$$

Now, solve the equation. Start by adding on the right side.

$$8n = 64$$

Then, divide both sides of the equation by 8.

$$n = 8$$

Therefore, the number 8 multiplied by 8 is 5 more than 59.

18. C: To compare the fractions, express them with a common denominator. This is done by multiplying each fraction's numerator and denominator by the denominator of the other. Therefore, $\frac{2}{3} \times \frac{4}{4} = \frac{8}{12}$, and $\frac{3}{4} \times \frac{3}{3} = \frac{9}{12}$. The correct answer must lie between these two numbers. Since $\frac{8}{12} = \frac{16}{24}$, and $\frac{9}{12} = \frac{18}{24}$, the fraction $\frac{17}{24}$ is between these two numbers and is correct.

19. B: Each prism has five faces: identical top and bottom triangular bases and three rectangular lateral faces. Each base is a right triangle, so its area is half the product of its legs. Each lateral face is a rectangle whose length is a side of the triangular base and whose width is the height of the prism. So, the bases of prism A each have area $\frac{1}{2} \cdot 3 \cdot 4 = 6 \text{ cm}^2$, and the bases of prism B each have area $\frac{1}{2} \cdot 5 \cdot 12 = 30 \text{ cm}^2$. The lateral faces of prism A have areas $3 \times 20 = 60 \text{ cm}^2$, $4 \times 20 = 80 \text{ cm}^2$, and $5 \times 20 = 100 \text{ cm}^2$. The lateral faces of prism B have areas $5 \times h = 5h \text{ cm}^2$, $12 \times h = 12h \text{ cm}^2$, and $13 \times h = 13h \text{ cm}^2$, where h is the unknown height of prism B. So, the surface area of prism A is $6 + 6 + 60 + 80 + 100 = 252 \text{ cm}^2$, and the surface area of prism B is $30 + 30 + 5h + 12h + 13h = 60 + 30h \text{ cm}^2$. We want to have $60 + 30h > 252$. Subtracting 60 from both sides of the inequality gives us $30h > 192$, and dividing by 30 yields $h > \frac{192}{30} = \frac{32}{5} = 6\frac{2}{5}$ cm. The smallest such whole number is $h = 7$ cm.

20. A: Find the value of each expression.

$$0.8 \times 0.7 = 0.56$$
$$0.08 \times 0.07 = 0.0056$$
$$0.008 \times 0.007 = 0.000056$$

Therefore, the statement (I) > (II) > (III) is true.

21. C: In this sequence, each term is equal to 12 less than the previous term. For example, $1{,}999 - 12 = 1{,}987$ and $1{,}987 - 12 = 1{,}975$. Therefore, the following term must be equal to $1{,}975 - 12 = 1{,}963$.

22. B: Each term in the sequence is equal to 5 raised to a power equal to its position in the sequence. For example, the third term is equal to $5^3 = 125$.

23. D: If Tyler's age is T and Clay's age is C, then $T + C = 21$ and $T = 3C + 1$. Rearrange the first equation to get C in terms of T.

$$C = 21 - T$$

Then, substitute the second equation and solve for T.

$$\begin{aligned} T &= 3(21 - T) + 1 \\ T &= 63 - 3T + 1 \\ T &= 64 - 3T \\ 4T &= 64 \\ T &= 16 \end{aligned}$$

Therefore, Tyler is 16 years old.

24. A: The volume of a cube is its edge length cubed (that is, its edge length to the third power), so the volume of the cube is $V = 4^3 = 64$ cubic feet. The volume of a box is the product of its length, width, and height, so the volume of this box is $V = 7 \times 4 \times 2 = 56$ cubic feet. Thus, the cube has the larger volume. The surface area of a cube is the sum of the areas of its six square faces. In this cube, the faces are squares with edges of length 4 feet, so the area of each face is $4 \times 4 = 16$ square feet, and the surface area of the cube is $SA = 6 \times 16 = 96$ square feet. The surface area of a box is the sum of the areas of its six rectangular faces. This box has two faces with an area of $7 \times 4 = 28$ square feet, two faces with an area of $7 \times 2 = 14$ square feet, and two faces with an area of $4 \times 2 = 8$ square feet. Thus, the surface area of the box is $2 \times 28 + 2 \times 14 + 2 \times 8 = 56 + 28 + 16 = 100$ square feet. So, the box has the larger surface area.

25. A: According to the associative property of multiplication, a product can be grouped in different ways and have the same value. Therefore, all three statements are equal, and the statement (I) = (II) = (III) is true.

26. A: Rewrite the answer choices with equal numerators and compare the denominators.

$$\frac{1}{3} = \frac{1 \times 100}{3 \times 100} = \frac{100}{300}$$
$$\frac{10}{33} = \frac{10 \times 10}{33 \times 10} = \frac{100}{330}$$

Since all the numerators are the same, the fraction with the smallest denominator is the largest. Therefore, $\frac{1}{3}$ is the greatest.

27. B: In this sequence, each term is double the previous term. For example, $7 \times 2 = 14$, and $14 \times 2 = 28$. The next term must be $56 \times 2 = 112$.

28. A: Convert all the fractions to a common denominator of 16.

$$\frac{1}{2} = \frac{1 \times 8}{2 \times 8} = \frac{8}{16}$$
$$\frac{3}{8} = \frac{3 \times 2}{8 \times 2} = \frac{6}{16}$$
$$\frac{7}{16} = \frac{7}{16}$$
$$\frac{13}{52} = \frac{13 \div 13}{52 \div 13} = \frac{1}{4} = \frac{1 \times 4}{4 \times 4} = \frac{4}{16}$$

The largest numerator is 8, so the largest fraction is $\frac{1}{2}$.

29. C: The volume of a cube is the cube (third power) of its edge length. Let e be the edge length of the small cube. Then the volume of the small cube is $V = e^3$. The edge length of the large cube is $1.5e$ (50% greater than the small cube), so the large cube has volume $V = (1.5e)^3 = 1.5^3e^3 = 3.375e^3$. Thus, the volume of the large cube is 3.375 times that of the small cube (between 3 and 4 times that of the small cube).

30. C: Write out the statement as an expression.

$$(13 \times 7) + 12$$

Now, simplify using the order of operations. First, multiply 13 by 7.

$$91 + 12$$

Then, add the two numbers.

$$91 + 12 = 103$$

31. C: The terms increase by 8 each time, therefore, the sequence is arithmetic. Use the nth term formula for arithmetic sequences to determine the 16th term.

$$a_n = a_1 + (n-1)d$$
$$a_{15} = 2 + (16-1)(8)$$
$$a_{15} = 2 + (15)(8)$$
$$a_{15} = 2 + 120$$
$$a_{15} = 122$$

The 15th term in the sequence is 122.

32. D: To find this number, set up an equation where n is the value of the unknown number.

$$n \div 2 = \frac{2}{3} \times 66$$

Now, solve the equation for n. Start by multiplying on the right side of the equation.

$$n \div 2 = 44$$

Then, multiply by 2 on both sides.

$$n = 88$$

Therefore, the number is 88.

33. D: If both numbers are positive and the greater one is subtracted from the smaller, the result must be less than zero, or negative. There is not enough information given to determine if it is even or odd.

34. D: The pattern is subtracting one less than the previous time, starting with subtracting 9.

$$132 - 9 = 123$$
$$123 - 8 = 115$$
$$115 - 7 = 108$$
$$108 - 6 = 102$$

The next number to be subtracted is 5.

$$102 - 5 = 97$$

Therefore, the next number in the sequence is 97.

35. C: In this sequence, the interval between successive numbers increases by an amount that is one less than the previous interval.

$$23 - 18 = 5$$
$$27 - 23 = 4$$
$$33 - 32 = 1$$

Therefore, the next number should be $27 + 3$, or 30.

36. A: The common ratio refers to the amount that each term in a sequence is multiplied by to generate the next term in the sequence. In this case, each term is multiplied by 3. The common ratio is 3.

37. C: The product of two odd numbers must be odd. The product of a positive number and a negative number must be negative. Therefore, this product is odd and negative.

38. C: A number less than zero is a negative number, and the product of two negative numbers must be positive. We are not able to tell if the result will be even or odd based on the given information.

39. D: The point $(7, y)$ represents the eighth point in this sequence. The value of each y-value in the sequence is equal to the point's position in the sequence times 3. Thus, the corresponding y-value equals 8×3, or 24.

40. D: Even numbers must be integers, so the result cannot be a fraction. Only one even number, 2, is prime, so the result cannot be prime. The product of any number and an even number must be even, so the result cannot be odd, and choice D must be correct.

41. D: Since "percent" means "parts per 100", 90% is equal to $\frac{90}{100} = \frac{9}{10}$. The decimal expression 0.9 is also equal to $\frac{9}{10}$, so (I) and (III) are equal. However, $\frac{1}{9} \neq \frac{9}{10}$, so the statement (I) = (III) ≠ (II) is correct.

42. C: The nth term formula for geometric sequences is $a_n = a_1 r^{(n-1)}$.

a_n represents the nth term in the sequence.

a_1 represents the first term in the sequence.

r represents the common ratio.

n represents the position of the term.

43. D: Find the value of each expression. Following normal order of operations, the expressions within the parentheses must be evaluated first.

$$(3 \times 4) + 5 = 12 + 5 = 17$$
$$(4 + 5) \times 6 = 9 \times 6 = 54$$
$$(3 \times 5) + 6 = 15 + 6 = 21$$

Therefore, the statement (I) < (II) and (II) > (III) is true.

44. C: The circumference, C, of a circle is given by the formula $C = 2\pi r$, where r is the radius of the circle and π is a constant approximately equal to 3.14. Thus, the circumference of the circle is $C = 2\pi(5) = 10\pi \approx 10 \times 3.14 = 31.4$ feet. The perimeter of a square is 4 times the edge length (since all four sides are equal); so, the smallest whole-number edge length that gives the square a perimeter greater than 31.4 feet is 8 feet (since $4 \times 8 = 32 > 31.4$ but $4 \times 7 = 28 < 31.4$).

45. D: The area of a circle is πr^2, where r is the radius, so the area of circle A is $\pi \times 3^2 = 9\pi$ square meters. Since the value of π is about 3.1, we see that 9π is about $9 \times 3.1 = 27.9$ square meters. The area of a rectangle is length times width, so the area of rectangle B is $13 \times 2 = 26$ square meters. The area of a square is its edge length squared, so the area of square C is $6^2 = 36$ square meters. So, rectangle B has the smallest area (26 square meters), followed by circle A (about 27.9 square meters) and square C (36 square meters).

46. C: A prime number can be factored only by itself and by 1. Since the product of two prime numbers can be factored by either of the primes, it cannot be prime itself. The product of two prime numbers will not always be odd or negative.

47. B: The product of any number and an even number must be even. Therefore, the first product will be even. The second multiplication produces the product of this even number and an odd number, which must also be even. Therefore, the final result must be even.

48. D: The surface area of a cube is the sum of the areas of its 6 square faces. The area of a square is its edge length squared. Since the faces of the cube are squares with edge length 4 cm, the area of each face is $4^2 = 16$ square centimeters. Thus, the surface area of the cube is $6 \times 16 = 96$ square centimeters. So, we want the smallest square (with a whole-number edge length) whose area exceeds 96 square centimeters. Since $9^2 = 81 < 96$ and $10^2 = 100 > 96$, we see that the smallest square whose area exceeds 96 square centimeters has an edge length of 10 cm.

49. C: In this sequence, each term is equal to 3 added to the previous term. For example, $-9 + 3 = -6, -6 + 3 = -3$, and $-3 + 3 = 0$. Therefore, the following term must be equal to $0 + 3$, which is 3.

50. A: Together angles 1 and 2 span one side of a straight line (they form a "straight angle"), and thus together they add up to 180°. Since the measure of angle 1 is 90°, the measure of angle 2 is $180° - 90° = 90°$. Thus, the two angles are equal.

51. D: The numbers in this sequence progress according to a pattern. Each progressing number can be expressed by the equation $x + 2 = n$, where x is the difference between the previous two numbers and n is the number added to the previous number, to yield the progressing number. For instance, the difference in 24 and 16 is 8. By adding 2 to 8, you know that you must add 10 to 24 in order to yield 34. In the next part of the sequence, $x = 10$ and $n = 12$. $34 + 12 = 46$, the next number in the sequence. Therefore, by following this pattern, you would add 16 to 60, which results in 76.

52. D: Evaluate each expression.

$$(-4) - 10 = -14$$
$$(-25) - (-30) = 5$$
$$4 \times (-20) = -80$$
$$-2 \times (-10) = 20$$

The value 20 is greatest, which means the expression $4 \times (-20)$ is greatest.

Mathematics

1. B: Use the order of operations when simplifying this expression. The acronym PEMDAS represents the correct order: parentheses, exponents, multiplication and division, addition and subtraction.

$$4(6 - 3)^2 - (-2)$$

First, simplify the parentheses.

$$4(3)^2 - (-2)$$

Next, simplify the exponent.

$$4 \times 9 - (-2)$$

Then multiply.

$$36 - (-2)$$

Finally, subtract.

$$36 - (-2) = 36 + 2 = 38$$

2. B: The difference between 76 °C and -18 °C is $76 - (-18) = 76 + 18 = 94$ °C. This is the total number of degrees Celsius that you must lower the temperature of the corn to reach your goal. When the temperature of the corn is half this amount, namely $\frac{94}{2} = 47$ °C, you are halfway to your goal.

3. D: To find how far Rafael travels, multiply the average speed by the elapsed time: $2.5 \times 36 = 90$. He travels 90 miles.

4. C: Determine how much of the candle has been consumed by subtracting its present length from its original length: $21 \text{ cm} - 9 \text{ cm} = 12 \text{ cm}$. Since the candle is consumed at the rate of 3 cm per hour, divide the length that has been consumed by this rate to obtain the time it has been burning: $\frac{12}{3} = 4$. The candle has been burning for 4 hours.

5. D: To simplify the expression, use the exponent rule $(x^m)^n = x^{m \times n}$.

$$(3x^{-2})^3 = (3)^3 (x^{-2})^3 = 27x^{-6}$$

6. D: If x is the cost of the pen, then, $2x$ is the cost of the book and $4x$ is the cost of the calculator. Vivian has spent $x + 2x + 4x$, or $7x$. She started with \$50 and had \$15 left, so $\$50 - 7x = \$15$. Solving for x, $x = \frac{\$50-\$15}{7} = \frac{\$35}{7} = \$5$, and the cost of the calculator was $4x = 4(\$5) = \$20$.

7. B: The volume of a rectangular box can be determined using the formula $V = l \times w \times h$, where l is the length of the box, w is the width of the box, and h is the height of the box. Therefore, the volume of the box described in this question is equal to $5 \times 7 \times 9$, or 315 in^3.

8. D: Use inverse operations to solve the inequality. Begin by adding 12 to both sides.

$$4x - 12 < 4$$
$$4x - 12 + 12 < 4 + 12$$
$$4x < 16$$

Then, divide both sides by 4.

$$\frac{4x}{4} < \frac{16}{4}$$
$$x < 4$$

Therefore, the solution to the inequality is $x < 4$.

9. B: Use the order of operations to find the value for this expression. The order of operations is: parentheses, exponents, multiplication and division, addition and subtraction.

$$-3 \times 5^2 + 2(4 - 18) + 33$$
$$= -3 \times 5^2 + 2(-14) + 33$$
$$= -3 \times 25 + 2(-14) + 33$$
$$= -75 + (-28) + 33$$
$$= -70$$

The value of the expression is –70.

10. B: Since $\frac{3}{5}$ of the vehicles are trucks, the remaining vehicles comprise $1 - \frac{3}{5} = \frac{2}{5}$ of the fleet. Since the entire fleet is 60 vehicles, $\frac{2}{5} \times 60 = 24$ vehicles are compact cars. One-half of these will be replaced by hybrids, or $\frac{24}{2} = 12$.

11. C: Note that a gain of 10% is the same as multiplying by 1.1 and a loss of 10% is the same as multiplying by 0.9. First, find the amount of money he has after adding 10% to his total.

$$1.1 \times 1{,}000 = 1{,}100$$

Then, find out how much money he has after he takes away 10% of this new amount.

$$0.9 \times 1{,}100 = 990$$

The man now has $990.

12. A: A triangular pyramid has four triangular faces. The arrangement of these faces in a two-dimensional figure is a net of a triangular pyramid if the figure can be folded to form a triangular pyramid. Choice B represents a rectangular pyramid, choice C is a triangular prism, and choice D is a square pyramid.

13. D: Relation D is the only one in which there is not any x-value that is mapped to more than one y-value. Thus, this relation represents a function.

14. C: The median of a set of numbers is one for which the set contains an equal number of greater and lesser values. Besides Z, there are 8 numbers in the set, so there must be 4 values greater than Z and 4 values less than Z. The 4 smallest values are 5, 7, 9, and 12. The 4 largest are 16, 18, 23, and 44, so Z must fall between 12 and 16. Therefore, the correct answer choice is 14.

15. C: The result for each toss is independent of the results for any other toss. For a single coin, the probability of tossing heads is $\frac{1}{2}$. For all three coins to come up heads, the probability is the product of the probabilities for each individual trial, or $P = \frac{1}{2} \times \frac{1}{2} \times \frac{1}{2} = \frac{1}{8}$.

16. B: Since the two lines are parallel, it follows that the angles δ and θ are equal. The angles α and θ are supplementary angles. That is, they add up to 180°. It follows that:

$$\theta = 180° - \alpha = 180° - 135° = 45°$$

Since $\delta = \theta$, then $\delta = 45°$.

17. B: Kevin has 12 shirts in all. The chance of selecting a blue shirt is $\frac{2}{12}$, since 2 of the shirts are blue. Likewise, the chance of selecting a red shirt is $\frac{4}{12}$, since 4 of the shirts are red. The probability of selecting either red or blue is the sum of these two probabilities: $\frac{2}{12} + \frac{4}{12} = \frac{6}{12} = \frac{1}{2}$, which is equal to 50%.

18. C: Tom's total at the end of the year will consist of the interest earned added to the original amount, or principal, that he deposited. The interest is 7% of $3,800.

$$7\% \times 3{,}800 = 0.07 \times 3{,}800 = 266$$

The amount of interest earned is $266. Adding this amount to the original amount deposited, $3,800, yields a total of $4,066.

19. A: The total cost consists of the price, the tax, and the shipping. First, calculate the 10% tax, which is $0.1 \times \$22 = \$2.20$. Add together all the elements of the cost: $\$22 + \$2.20 + \$4 = \$28.20$.

20. B: Following the order of operations, evaluate the expressions in the inner-most grouping symbols first, then work outward.

$$\begin{aligned}&15 + (16 - [2(11 - 6)] - 3)\\&= 15 + (16 - [2(5)] - 3)\\&= 15 + (16 - 10 - 3)\\&= 15 + 3\\&= 18\end{aligned}$$

The expression is equal to 18.

21. D: The percent change can be found using the following formula.

$$\%\text{ Change} = \frac{\text{new} - \text{old}}{\text{old}} \times 100$$

The old value is his current rent (750), and the new value is his new monthly rent (900).

$$\begin{aligned}\%\text{ Change} &= \frac{900 - 750}{750} \times 100\\\%\text{ Change} &= \frac{150}{750} \times 100\\\%\text{ Change} &= \frac{1}{5} \times 100\\\%\text{ Change} &= 20\end{aligned}$$

Since the percent change is positive, this represents a percent increase of 20%.

22. A: Apply the rules for exponents $(x^m)^n = x^{m \cdot n}$ and $x^m \cdot x^n = x^{m+n}$.

$$\begin{aligned}(x^2)^3 \cdot (y^2)^5 \cdot (y^4)^3 &= (x^{2\cdot 3}) \cdot (y^{2\cdot 5}) \cdot (y^{4\cdot 3})\\&= x^6 \cdot y^{10} \cdot y^{12}\\&= x^6 \cdot y^{10+12}\\&= x^6y^{22}\end{aligned}$$

The simplified expression is x^6y^{22}.

23. D: The graph shows five days that Jen runs. On three of the days (Tuesday, Thursday, and Friday), she runs four or more miles. So three out of five days, or $\frac{3}{5}$ of the time, she runs at least four miles.

24. C: To multiply and divide fractions with mixed numbers, first convert the mixed number to an improper fraction. The mixed number $1\frac{1}{8}$ becomes the improper fraction $\frac{9}{8}$.

$$\frac{1}{4} \times \frac{3}{5} \div \frac{9}{8}$$

Simplify the expression by using the order of operations. Multiply and divide in order from left to right: $\frac{1}{4} \times \frac{3}{5} = \frac{3}{20}$.

$$\frac{3}{20} \div \frac{9}{8}$$

Then, simplify the division, which requires multiplying by the inverse of the second fraction.

$$\frac{3}{20} \div \frac{9}{8} = \frac{3}{20} \times \frac{8}{9} = \frac{24}{180}$$

This result simplifies to $\frac{2}{15}$.

25. C: Since 1 meter equals 100 centimeters, the conversion factor is 100. Since a centimeter is shorter than a meter, we divide by the conversion factor.

$$7{,}200 \text{ cm} \times \frac{1 \text{ m}}{100 \text{ cm}} = 72 \text{ m}$$

Therefore, 7,200 centimeters is equivalent to 72 meters.

26. D: Start by isolating a on one side of the equation.

$$a - 16 = 8b + 6$$
$$a = 8b + 6 + 16$$
$$a = 8b + 22$$

Next, add 3 to both side of the equation.

$$a + 3 = 8b + 22 + 3$$
$$a + 3 = 8b + 25$$

27. A: The distance given from the top to the bottom of the tire through the center is the diameter. Finding the distance the bike traveled in one complete roll of the tire is the same as finding the circumference. Using the formula, $C = \pi d$, we multiply 27 by π, so $C = 27\pi$. From the first mark to the fourth, the tire rolls three times. Then, you would multiply by 3, and the distance would be $3(27\pi)$.

28. B: The odds of a black balloon being chosen at random from a bag of balloons is calculated using the following formula.

$$P = \frac{\text{\# black balloons}}{\text{\# total balloons}}$$

The total number of balloons is found by adding up the number of each color.

$$37 + 8 + 15 = 60$$

There are 15 black balloons, so calculate the probability of selecting a black balloon.

$$P = \frac{15}{60} = 25\%$$

The probability that a balloon chosen randomly will be black is 25%.

29. C: Add each of the changes to the original percentage.

$$\begin{aligned}&35\% + (-2\%) + (-1\%) + (+6\%) + (-1\%) + (+2\%)\\&= 35\% + 2\% + 6\% - 2\% - 1\% - 1\%\\&= 43\% - 4\%\\&= 39\%\end{aligned}$$

The percentage of sales in electronics at the end of 2005 is 39%.

30. C: Solve the equation using inverse operations. First, subtract 5 from both sides.

$$\begin{aligned}3x + 5 &= 11\\3x + 5 - 5 &= 11 - 5\\3x &= 6\end{aligned}$$

Then, divide both sides by 3.

$$\begin{aligned}\frac{3x}{3} &= \frac{6}{3}\\x &= 2\end{aligned}$$

Therefore, the value of x is 2.

31. A: Since 1 foot equals 12 inches, the conversion factor is $\frac{12 \text{ in}}{1 \text{ ft}}$. Multiply by the conversion factor.

$$4 \text{ ft} \times \frac{12 \text{ in}}{1 \text{ ft}} = 48 \text{ in}$$

Therefore, there are 48 inches in 4 feet.

32. B: To find out how much money Sandra already has, subtract how much she needs from the total cost of the book.

$$12 - 3 = 9$$

Therefore, Sandra has $9.

33. D: The average temperature in October is 26°C, and in November it is 16°C, a difference of 10°C. This is the steepest decline on the graph.

34. C: Six hours is equal to $6 \times 60 = 360$ minutes. If Alice can create 1 ring in 12 minutes, then in 360 minutes she can create $\frac{360}{12} = 30$ rings.

Here is another way to solve the problem. A rate of 1 ring in 12 minutes is equivalent to a rate of $\frac{1 \text{ ring}}{12 \text{ minutes}} \times \frac{60 \text{ minutes}}{1 \text{ hour}} = \frac{5 \text{ rings}}{1 \text{ hour}}$. Therefore, in 6 hours Alice can create $5 \times 6 = 30$ rings.

35. C: Divide the total in Andrea's account at the end of the year by the total number of deposits: $\frac{\$1{,}560}{52 \text{ weeks}} = \$30$ per week. This is the amount she saved each week. Since this amount represents

10% of her paycheck, $10\% = \frac{10}{100} = \frac{1}{10}$, and dividing by a fraction is the same as multiplying by the reciprocal: $\$30 \times 10 = \$300$. Therefore, her weekly paycheck is \$300.

36. D: Solve using conversion fractions. First, convert the mixed number to an improper fraction.

$$5\frac{1}{3}\text{yd} = \frac{16}{3}\text{ yd}$$

Now, convert from yards to inches.

$$\frac{16}{3}\text{ yd} \times \frac{36\text{ in}}{1\text{ yd}} = \frac{576}{3}\text{in} = 192\text{ in}$$

Then, convert from inches to centimeters.

$$192\text{ in} \times \frac{2.54\text{ cm}}{1\text{ in}} = 487.68\text{ cm}$$

Therefore, there are 487.68 centimeters in $5\frac{1}{3}$ yards.

37. C: Since each brother receives \$15, multiply 15 by 2.

$$15 \times 2 = 30$$

The total amount of the prize was \$30.

38. C: The ratio of left- to right-handed players will be the same as the ratio 2 : 3. Therefore, $\frac{2}{3} = \frac{12}{R}$, so that $R = 18$ right-handed players. The total number of girls on the roster is therefore $12 + 18 = 30$.

39. A: The frequency table in choice A correctly shows the frequencies represented by the histogram. The frequencies of values falling between 1 and 10 is 3, between 11 and 20 is 9, between 21 and 30 is 8, between 31 and 40 is 6, and between 41 and 50 is 4.

40. D: You would write the negative square root of 100 as $-\sqrt{100}$.

41. C: Hiking due west at 3 mph, the first hiker will have gone 6 miles after 2 hours. Hiking due north at 4 mph, the second hiker will have gone 8 miles after 2 hours. Since one hiker headed west and the other headed north, their distance from each other can be drawn as:

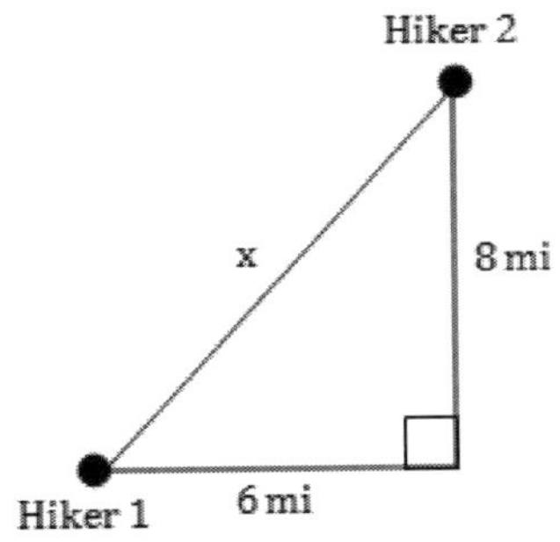

Since the distance between the two hikers is the hypotenuse of a right triangle, and since we know the lengths of the two legs of the right triangle, we can use the Pythagorean theorem $(a^2 + b^2 = c^2)$ to find the value of x.

$$6^2 + 8^2 = x^2$$
$$36 + 64 = x^2$$
$$100 = x^2$$
$$10 = x$$

Therefore, the hikers are 10 miles apart after 2 hours of hiking.

42. A: Prime factors are prime numbers that can be multiplied together to give the number in question. A prime number is a number that can be factored only by itself and by 1. To factor 93, divide by the first available prime that is greater than 1. Since the number is not divisible by 2, divide by 3: $93 = 3 \times 31$. Since 31 is also a prime number, the process can be taken no further, and the number 93 has only 2 prime factors.

43. C: If the perimeter is 44 cm, then the side of the square $s = \frac{P}{4} = \frac{44}{4} = 11$. Since the area of a square $A = s^2$, then $A = 11^2 = 11 \times 11 = 121$. Therefore, the area of a square with a perimeter of 44 cm is 121 cm^2.

44. D: For Days 1, 2, and 3 (choices A, B, and C) on the chart, the number of seedlings is 0. Day 4 is the first time we see the line move away from 0, showing that 2 seedlings sprouted that day.

45. B: One side of a square is 56 cm. All of its sides are equal, and the perimeter is the sum of all sides.

$$56 \text{ cm} + 56 \text{ cm} + 56 \text{ cm} + 56 \text{ cm} = 224 \text{ cm}$$

Therefore, the perimeter is 224 cm.

46. A: A function is a relation in which there is not any x-value that is mapped to more than one y-value. The only relation that represents a function is $\{(2,1), (3,-2), (6,8), (-1,-4), (4,-1)\}$.

47. D: Since there are 12 inches in a foot, then 4 inches is equal to $\frac{4}{12} = \frac{1}{3}$ foot. This means that 3 feet 4 inches is equivalent to $3\frac{1}{3}$ feet.

48. C: It is helpful to recall that percentages can be converted to decimals. 30% of 3,300 is $0.3 \times 3{,}300 = 990$. Therefore, the crane supports 990 pounds.

49. B: Remember the order of operations: parentheses, exponents, multiplication and division, addition and subtraction.

Perform the operations inside the parentheses first.

$$5(10) + (5) - (45)$$

Then, do any multiplication and division, working from left to right. Remember, a number next to parentheses tells you to multiply the two values.

$$50 + 5 - 45$$

Finally, do any adding or subtracting, working from left to right.

$$55 - 45 = 10$$

50. A: Converting from one metric unit to another requires moving the decimal point to the left or right. The table below shows the prefixes of some common metric units.

Prefix	kilo-	hecto-	deka-		deci-	centi-	milli-
Symbol	k	h	da		d	c	m
Unit Measure	10^3	10^2	10^1	$10^0 = 1$	10^{-1}	10^{-2}	10^{-3}

The difference in powers of 10 shows us how many places to move the decimal point. Since the decigram is four places to the right of the kilogram in the table, we can move the decimal point in 14.75 kg four places to the right to convert it to decigrams. Inserting two zeros after 14.75, we get:

$$14.\underset{\smile}{7}\,\underset{\smile}{5}\,\underset{\smile}{0}\,\underset{\smile}{0}. = 147{,}500$$

So, 14.75 kg = 147,500 dg.

51. B: "Bisect" means to divide exactly in half. Therefore, the measure of $\angle BAD$ is twice as large as the measure of $\angle BAC$. Since $2 \times 15 = 30$, the measure of $\angle BAD$ is 30°.

52. B: On a dot plot, each dot (or "x"), represents one response. Here, we're trying to determine how many students watched more than 8 hours of television over the weekend. "More than 8" tells us to only include students who responded with 9 or 10 hours because 9 and 10 are the only numbers on the graph that are greater than 8. We can't include the students who responded exactly 8 hours because 8 is not greater than 8 (8 is equal to 8). We can see that 3 students reported watching 9 hours of television, while 5 say they watched 10 hours of television. The sum of 3 and 5 is 8, which means 8 students watched more than 8 hours of television this weekend.

53. B: The given angles are alternate interior angles. According to the alternate interior angles theorem, when a transversal cuts across parallel lines, the alternate interior angles are congruent. Since lines a and b are parallel, it means that the two given angles are congruent. Solve the following equation for x.

$$2x + 5 = 3x - 25$$
$$2x + 30 = 3x$$
$$30 = x$$

Therefore, the value of x is 30.

54. C: Use the order of operations to simplify this expression. First, simplify all operations inside parentheses.

$$2(7 + 8)^2 - 12(6 \times 2)$$
$$2(15)^2 - 12(12)$$

Second, simplify any exponential expressions.

$$2(225) - 12(12)$$

Third, perform all multiplication and division as they occur in the problem from left to right.

$$450 - 144$$

Fourth, perform all addition and subtraction as they occur in the problem from left to right.

$$450 - 144 = 306$$

The value of the expression is 306.

55. C: \$25 is equivalent to $100\% - 80\% = 20\%$ of the original price P. Since "percent" means "parts per 100", then $\frac{25}{P} = \frac{20}{100}$. To solve this proportion, multiply both sides by P and by 100, which yields $25 \times 100 = 20P$. Now, divide both sides of this equation by 20: $P = 125$. Therefore, the normal price of the game is \$125.

56. C: The numbers 12 and 8 are not prime numbers, so they cannot be prime factors of 121. 121 is not divisible by 13, so it is also incorrect. However, $11 \times 11 = 121$, and 11 is prime, so 11 is correct.

57. C: If 120 is $\frac{1}{4}$ less than yesterday's number, we can write this as: $120 = y - \frac{1}{4}y$, where y is yesterday's number. We combine terms on the right to solve: $120 = \frac{3}{4}y$, so $y = 120\left(\frac{4}{3}\right) = 160$. Therefore, 160 people purchased coffee yesterday.

58. C: Since "percent" means "parts per 100", cell phone users are $\frac{240}{100}$ times as likely to have tumors as other people, for whom the rate is 12 per 100,000. The answer is therefore $12 \times \frac{240}{100} = 28.8$ people per 100,000.

59. D: When there are two operations within our parentheses, we must follow the order of operations *within* the parentheses as well. Because multiplication comes before addition, we must start by finding the product of 4 and 3, which is 12. Next, we add 10 and 12 to get 22. Finally, we can divide 22 by 2 to arrive at our final answer, 11.

60. C: The area scales with the square of the radius, so if the radius increases in length by a factor of 2, the area will increase by 2^2, or 4. Since Area $= \pi r^2$, if the radius r is replaced with $2r$, this yields Area $= \pi(2r)^2 = 4\pi r^2$, which is 4 times the original area.

$$31 \times 4 = 124$$

Therefore, the area of the new circle is 124 square units.

61. C: Start by solving $5y - 20 < 0$ for y.

$$\begin{aligned} 5y - 20 &< 0 \\ 5y &< 20 \\ y &< 4 \end{aligned}$$

Since y must be an integer, the answer must be 3 because 3 is the largest integer that is less than 4.

62. B: The two right triangles are similar because they share a pair of vertical angles. Vertical angles are always congruent (e.g., $\angle ACB$ and $\angle DCE$). Both right angles (e.g., $\angle B$ and $\angle D$) are also congruent. So, $\angle A$ and $\angle E$ are congruent because of the triangular sum theorem.

With similar triangles, corresponding sides will be proportional. $\overline{BC}$ is $\frac{1}{2}$ the length of $\overline{CD}$. So, $\overline{AC}$ will be $\frac{1}{2}$ the length of $\overline{CE}$. The length of $\overline{CE}$ can be computed from the Pythagorean theorem because it is the hypotenuse of a right triangle where the lengths of the other two sides are known.

$$\overline{CE} = \sqrt{6^2 + 8^2} = \sqrt{36 + 64} = \sqrt{100} = 10$$

The length of $\overline{AC}$ will be $\frac{1}{2}$ of this value, or 5 units.

63. D: Since a pound equals 16 ounces, the conversion factor is $\frac{1 \text{ lb}}{16 \text{ oz}}$. Multiply by the conversion factor.

$$32 \text{ oz} \times \frac{1 \text{ lb}}{16 \text{ oz}} = 2 \text{ lb}$$

Therefore, 32 ounces is equivalent to 2 pounds.

64. D: The three-dimensional shape being described must be a pyramid because it only has one base and all triangular sides. We can envision the sides meeting at the top, forming the point of the pyramid. Furthermore, a pyramid is named for the shape of its base. Here, the pyramid has a square base so we must classify it as a square pyramid.

HSPT Practice Test #2

Reading—Comprehension

Refer to the following for questions 1–13:

The first photographs were based on the work of the German chemist Johann Heinrich Schulze who, in 1727, discovered that silver nitrate darkened upon exposure to light. The first "photograms" were images made by exposing silver nitrate on paper or metal surfaces. During the nineteenth century, a number of researchers worked to combine this effect with various lenses in order to capture and reproduce images from different sources. The first process for making commercial images was ultimately announced in 1839 by Louis Jacques Mandé Daguerre, a French painter whose name became attached to the product, the daguerreotype.

The daguerreotype quickly became popular in Victorian England, where it was used, principally, for portraits. Today, as photography moves beyond the chemical capture of images onto paper and into the digital era, other applications abound: landscapes, interiors, sports and journalism, to name but a few. And yet, the portrait remains one of the major applications for the technology.

In portraiture, as in other types of photography, the nature and characteristics of light are of the utmost importance. To the photographer, light is a living thing, dynamic and animated. But, whereas in sports or journalism, for example, the photographer must make do with the light conditions he finds when it is time to shoot, light can usually be controlled for a portrait shot. And, good lighting can make all the difference in the world in a portrait, conveying mood, revealing detail, establishing the photographer's style, even making a "mistake" seem like a bit of *panache*. Understanding light is the creative equivalent of a get-out-of-jail-free card. So much so that the professional portrait photographer expends a great deal of time and money on lights and equipment that will put him in charge.

The various lighted areas of a photograph are described as *highlights, mid-tones,* and *shadows. Specular* highlights are the brightest spots: direct reflections from the studio lights or strobes. In a portrait they are typically seen in the eyes or on the tip of the nose. From these bright portions, *diffused* highlights spread gradually into the mid-tones. At the other side of the mid-tonal range, there will be *transition areas* where the available light fades gradually into the dark shadows. If these transitions are abrupt, narrow areas, the lighting is said to be *hard light.* Hard light can give a stark effect to portraits and might be used for a craggy-faced coal miner, for example, or for black-and-white shots. Broader transitions produce *soft lighting*, and lead to a gentler mood. This type of lighting is more suitable for a wedding portrait, for example.

A wide variety of devices are available for producing and modifying the light in a photographic studio. Studio lighting has the advantage of being reproducible, so the skilled photographer can get the same results every time. Modern lighting usually consists of flash units, also called *strobes*, rather than the hot, power-hungry floodlights that used to be the norm. While this equipment can be elaborate and expensive, it doesn't have to be. A poor carpenter blames his tools, but with practice, one can get great results from a simple setup comprised of two or three lights. Studio lighting setups vary with the preferences of the photographer, but they all have a number of elements in common.

The main light that shines on the subject is called the *key light*. The camera exposure is determined by the amount of light the key throws upon the subject. The key is usually positioned off to one side of the camera, and will throw shadows across the face from the subject's nose and eyebrows. One or more *fill lights* may be used to lighten these shadowed areas and reduce image harshness. Fill lights are adjusted to throw half as much light, or less, onto the subject compared to the key. A *kicker* may be positioned to illuminate the back of the model, creating a halo effect and making the subject stand out from the background. Finally, there may be *background lights* to illuminate the background directly.

Studio photographers often use *modifiers* of one type or another to diffuse and soften the light emanating from these sources. Modifiers make the light source effectively larger, reducing shadows and broadening transition areas. The best-known light modifier is the photographer's white umbrella, which can be used to reflect light from the source onto the model, but many other types of modifiers exist. The simplest is a large piece of white cardboard, called a *fill card*. As with lights, the choice of modifiers is a matter of individual preference, and every studio photographer has his favorite combinations of lights and modifiers for achieving different effects.

Although the basic principles remain the same, the practice of photography has come a long way since the days of the daguerreotype.

1. The main purpose of this passage is:

a. To give a history of photography
b. To show that different photographers have different styles
c. To compare portraiture with other forms of photography
d. To give an overview of photographic portrait lighting

2. The main purpose of the first three paragraphs is to:

a. Explain how daguerreotypes were made
b. Describe the different kinds of photography
c. Provide context for the discussion of portrait lighting
d. Contrast chemical and digital photography

3. The word "photogram" (Line 5) is between quotation marks because:

a. It is something that Johann Heinrich Schulze said.
b. It is a coined term not in common use today.
c. It is a German word.
d. The author wants to place emphasis upon it.

4. The phrase "light is a living thing" (Line 30) is an example of:

a. A metaphor
b. A simile
c. An exaggeration
d. An anthropomorphism

5. The word "mistake" (Line 40) is between quotation marks because:

a. It is something that someone said
b. It is a slang expression
c. It describes something that may not really be an error
d. All photographers make mistakes sometimes

6. The phrase "Understanding light is the creative equivalent of a get-out-of-jail-free card" (Lines 41–42) is an example of:

a. A metaphor
b. A simile
c. An attribution
d. Poetic license

7. The main purpose of paragraph 4 is to:

a. Show the relationship between lighting and mood
b. Explain the difference between hard and soft light
c. Tell the reader what kind of lighting to use for a wedding portrait
d. Define a number of terms used to describe lighting features on photographs

8. The word "specular" (Line 49) is in italics because:

a. It is a term that is being defined in the sentence
b. It is a foreign word
c. It is misspelled
d. It is a slang expression

9. The sentence that describes floodlights as hot and power-hungry implies that flash units, or strobes,...

a. are also hot and power-hungry.
b. are more modern than floodlights.
c. are more expensive than floodlights.
d. are not hot or power-hungry.

10. The words "model" and "subject":

a. Refer to the same thing
b. Contrast two different things that may be photographed
c. Contrast the front and back of the person being photographed
d. Are both conjunctions

11. The main purpose of paragraph 6 is to:

a. Describe how to set the camera exposure
b. Tell the reader where to position a key light
c. Define the different types of studio lights
d. Distinguish between floodlights and strobes

12. The main purpose of paragraph 7 is to:

a. Tell the reader how to use an umbrella
b. Explain the use of white cardboard in photography
c. Show how to make strobes brighter
d. Describe ways to soften the light that comes from studio strobes or floodlights

13. After reading this passage, readers should understand:

a. Why portraits were popular in Victorian England
b. The complexity of photographic portrait lighting
c. Why camera equipment is so expensive
d. Exactly how to position lights for portrait photography

Refer to the following for questions 14–18:

From 1892 to 1954, over twelve million immigrants entered the United States through the portal of Ellis Island, a small island in New York Harbor. Ellis Island is located in the upper bay just off the New Jersey coast, within the shadow of the Statue of Liberty. Through the years, this gateway to the new world was enlarged from its original 3.3 acres to 27.5 acres by landfill supposedly obtained from the ballast of ships, excess earth from the construction of the New York City subway system and elsewhere.

Before being designated as the site of one of the first Federal immigration station by President Benjamin Harrison in 1890, Ellis Island had a varied history. The local Indian tribes had called it "Kioshk" or Gull Island. Due to its rich and abundant oyster beds and plentiful and profitable shad runs, it was known as Oyster Island for many generations during the Dutch and English colonial periods. By the time Samuel Ellis became the island's private owner in the 1770's, the island had been called Kioshk, Oyster, Dyre, Bucking and Anderson's Island. In this way, Ellis Island developed from a sandy island that barely rose above the high tide mark, into a hanging site for pirates, a harbor fort, ammunition and ordinance depot named Fort Gibson, and finally into an immigration station.

14. Which of the following is true about Ellis Island?

I. It houses the Statue of Liberty.
II. The local Indian tribes called it Oyster Island.
III. It was expanded using dirt from the construction of the subway system.

a. I only
b. I and II only
c. II and III only
d. III only

15. The word "portal" in the first paragraph most likely means:

a. Island
b. Gateway
c. Boat
d. Subway

16. The style of this passage is most like that found in a(n):

a. Immigrant's diary
b. Business letter
c. History textbook
d. Persuasive essay

17. How did the island get its current name?

a. It was named after its private owner, Samuel Ellis.
b. It developed from a sandy island to an immigration station.
c. It was named after its abundant oyster beds.
d. It was an ordinance and ammunition depot.

18. The author probably included the different names of Ellis Island to show:

a. How many owners the island had
b. That pirates used the island
c. That its size was increased
d. The rich and varied history of the island

Refer to the following for questions 19–30:

The Coins of Ancient Greece

We don't usually think of coins as works of art, and most of them really do not invite us to do so. The study of coins, their development and history, is termed *numismatics*. Numismatics is a topic of great interest to archeologists and anthropologists, but not usually from the perspective of visual delectation. The coin is intended, after all, to be a utilitarian object, not an artistic one. Many early Greek coins are aesthetically pleasing as well as utilitarian, however, and not simply because they are the earliest examples of coin design. Rather, Greek civic individualism provides the reason. Every Greek political entity expressed its identity through its coinage.

The idea of stamping metal pellets of a standard weight with an identifying design had its origin on the Ionian Peninsula around 600 B.C. Each of the Greek city-states produced its own coinage adorned with its particular symbols. The designs were changed frequently to commemorate battles, treaties, and other significant occasions. In addition to their primary use as a pragmatic means of facilitating commerce, Greek coins were clearly an expression of civic pride. The popularity of early coinage led to a constant demand for new designs, such that there arose a class of highly skilled artisans who took great pride in their work, so much so that they sometimes even signed it. As a result, Greek coins provide us not only with an invaluable source of historical knowledge, but also with a genuine expression of the evolving Greek sense of form. These minuscule works reflect the development of Greek sculpture from the sixth to the second century B.C. as dependably as do larger works made of marble. And since they are stamped with the place and date of their production, they provide an historic record of artistic development that is remarkably dependable and complete.

19. What is the purpose of this passage?

a. To attract new adherents to numismatics as a pastime
b. To show how ancient Greeks used coins in commerce
c. To teach the reader that money was invented in Greece
d. To describe ancient Greek coinage as an art form

20. What is meant by the phrase "most of them really do not invite us to do so", as used in the first sentence?

a. Money is not usually included when sending an invitation.
b. Most coins are not particularly attractive.
c. Invitations are not generally engraved onto coins.
d. Coins do not speak.

21. What is a synonym for "delectation", as used in the third sentence?

a. Savoring
b. Choosing
c. Deciding
d. Refusing

22. What is meant by the term *numismatics*?

a. The study of numbers
b. Egyptian history
c. Greek history
d. The study of coins

23. According to the text, how do ancient Greek coins differ from most other coinage?

a. They are different simply because they were the first coins.
b. Each political entity made its own coins.
c. They were made of precious metals.
d. They were designed with extraordinary care.

24. How often were new coins designed in ancient Greece?

a. Monthly
b. Not very often.
c. Whenever there was a significant occasion to commemorate.
d. When the old ones wore out.

25. What is indicated by the fact that the artisans who designed the coins sometimes signed them?

a. They took pride in their work.
b. They were being held accountable for their work.
c. The signature certified the value of the coin.
d. The Greeks had developed writing.

26. What is meant by the term "pragmatic," as used in the third sentence of the second paragraph (Line 25)?

a. Valuable
b. Monetary
c. Useful
d. Practical

27. According to the passage, how are Greek coins similar to Greek sculpture?

a. Some sculptures were made of metal.
b. The coins were smaller.
c. Shapes were stamped into the coins.
d. Coin designs evolved along with the Greek sense of form.

28. Why is it significant that new coin designs were required frequently?

a. This indicates that there was a lot of commercial activity going on.
b. This gave the designers a lot of practice.
c. There were a lot of things to commemorate.
d. The Greeks needed to find new sources of precious metals.

29. **Why is it significant that the coins were dated, according to the passage?**
   a. The dates contributed to the designs.
   b. The age of the designers could be determined.
   c. It allows historians to track the evolution of Greek artistic styles.
   d. It allows historians to know when battles and treaties took place.

30. **What was the primary purpose of the Greek coin?**
   a. To commemorate treaties and battles.
   b. To provide minuscule works of art.
   c. They were used as adornments.
   d. To facilitate commerce.

Refer to the following for questions 31–40:

Annelids

The phylum Annelida, named for the Latin word *anellus*, meaning "ring," includes earthworms, leeches, and other similar organisms. In their typical form, these animals exhibit bilateral symmetry, a cylindrical cross section, and an elongate body divided externally into segments (*metameres*) by a series of rings (*annuli*). They are segmented internally as well, with most of the internal organs repeated in series in each segment. This organization is termed *metamerism*. Metameric segmentation is the distinguishing feature of this phylum, and provides it with a degree of evolutionary plasticity in that certain segments can be modified and specialized to perform specific functions. For example, in some species certain of the locomotor *parapodia*, or feet, may be modified for grasping, and some portions of the gut may evolve digestive specializations.

The gut is a straight, muscular tube that functions independently of the muscular activity in the body wall. The Annelida resemble the nematodes, another worm phylum, in possessing a fluid-filled internal cavity separating the gut from the body wall. In both phyla, this cavity is involved in locomotion. However, in the annelids, this space is formed at a much later time during the development of the embryo, and presumably evolved much later as well. This fluid-filled internal space is called a true *coelom*.

The annelid excretory and circulatory systems are well developed, and some members of the phylum have evolved respiratory organs. The nervous system offers a particular example of metameric specialization. It is concentrated anteriorly into enlarged cerebral ganglia connected to a ventral nerve cord that extends posteriorly and is organized into repeating segmental ganglia.

This phylum includes members bearing adaptations required for aquatic (marine or freshwater) or terrestrial habitats. They may be free-living entities or exist as parasites. Among the best known are the earthworm *Lumbricus*, the water leech *Hirudo*, and the marine worm *Nereis*.

31. **What is the purpose of this passage?**
   a. To describe the annelid nervous system
   b. To describe the annelid digestive system
   c. To introduce distinctive features of annelid anatomy
   d. To define metamerism

32. What is meant by the term *metamerism*?

a. Segmentation of the anatomy
b. A series of rings
c. Bilateral symmetry
d. Evolutionary plasticity

33. What is meant by the term *parapodia*?

a. Specialization
b. Grasping appendages
c. Locomotion
d. Feet

34. Which of the following is one evolutionary advantage of segmentation?

a. Segmented animals have many feet.
b. Segmented animals have a fluid-filled coelom.
c. Parts of some segments can become specialized to perform certain functions.
d. Segments can evolve.

35. A group of worms other than the Annelida are called:

a. Lumbricus
b. Nematodes
c. Leeches
d. Parapodia

36. The purpose of the last paragraph in the passage is to

a. give familiar examples of members of the annelid phylum.
b. show that annelids may be parasites.
c. tell the reader that annelids may be adapted to aquatic environments.
d. show that there are many annelids in nature and that they are adapted to a wide variety of habitats.

37. A difference between the annelid coelom and the fluid-filled cavity of other worms is that:

a. The annelid coelom is involved in locomotion.
b. The annelid coelom is formed later.
c. The annelid coelom is formed during embryology.
d. The annelid coelom is cylindrical in cross section.

38. An example of metameric specialization in the nervous system is:

a. Segmental ganglia
b. The ventral nerve cord
c. Respiratory organs
d. Cerebral ganglia

39. The main difference between the Annelida and all other animal phyla is that:

a. The Annelida are worms.
b. The Annelida include the leeches.
c. The Annelida are metameric.
d. The Annelida are aquatic.

40. The fluid-filled cavity in the nematodes is used for:

a. defense
b. reproduction
c. feeding
d. movement

Reading—Vocabulary

Refer to the following for questions 1–22:

Select the answer that is closest in meaning to the underlined portion.

1. The <u>defaced</u> statues

a. Restored
b. Vandalized
c. Intricate
d. Prominent

2. The woman <u>desired</u> a new car.

a. purchased
b. wanted
c. described
d. intended

3. Spanish is a difficult language to <u>comprehend</u>.

a. learn
b. speak
c. understand
d. appreciate

4. He <u>wandered</u> around the mall.

a. looked
b. shopped
c. roamed
d. searched

5. He is a very <u>courteous</u> young man.

a. handsome
b. polite
c. inconsiderate
d. odd

6. Her concern for him was <u>sincere</u>.

a. intense
b. genuine
c. brief
d. misunderstood

7. The <u>imminent</u> change

a. Royal
b. Painful
c. Unavoidable
d. Soon-to-occur

8. The math test was quite <u>challenging.</u>

a. reasonable
b. lengthy
c. difficult
d. simple

9. The workers <u>constructed</u> the home over a three-month period.

a. purchased
b. explored
c. improved
d. built

10. The <u>spare</u> tire

a. Small
b. Extra
c. Old
d. Flat

11. She is a very <u>intelligent</u> lady.

a. pretty
b. nice
c. smart
d. mysterious

12. The class <u>chuckled</u> when the professor dropped his notes.

a. helped
b. commented
c. laughed
d. chose

13. He <u>sprinted</u> down the road.

a. crawled
b. walked
c. hurried
d. ran

14. In the movie, the lead actress thought the lead actor was a burglar and <u>brandished</u> a stick at him in a threatening manner.

a. threw
b. waved menacingly
c. smacked
d. peered

15. He <u>observed</u> the eagles with binoculars.

a. watched
b. hunted
c. scared
d. sold

16. Our national <u>heritage</u>

a. Accent
b. Tradition
c. Pride
d. Income

17. Although they are not poisonous, pythons are able to hunt by <u>constricting</u> their prey with their long bodies.

a. expanded
b. narrowed
c. relaxed
d. unfolded

18. To <u>repudiate</u> under oath

a. Lie
b. Commit
c. Desist
d. Renounce

19. She attended the New Year's <u>festivities</u>.

a. commitments
b. celebrations
c. crowds
d. dates

20. Chefs can <u>enhance</u> the flavors of their dishes by adding seasonings and ingredients.

a. Complicate
b. Deteriorate
c. Diminish
d. Improve

21. The woman's performance was <u>superior</u> to the man's.

a. Short
b. Similar
c. Better
d. Weak

22. The <u>mulish</u> employee

a. Stubborn
b. Predictable
c. Unshaven
d. Impractical

Language

1. Identify the sentence that contains an error in usage, punctuation, or grammar. If no errors are found, choose the last option.

a. The first time I met my wife's father, I was very nervous.
b. The grocery list contained four items; lettuce, tomatoes, cheese, and milk.
c. John studied for his math test for three days straight.
d. No mistake.

2. Identify the sentence that contains an error in usage, punctuation, or grammar. If no errors are found, choose the last option.

a. Jill graduated at the top of her class.
b. Why does that car keep driving up and down the street?
c. Calculus is one of the most difficult school subjects.
d. No mistake.

3. Identify the sentence that contains an error in usage, punctuation, or grammar. If no errors are found, choose the last option.

a. The mountain turned out to be far higher than Jack had expected.
b. Last June was the hottest month of the year.
c. How long were you engaged before you got married.
d. No mistake.

4. Identify the sentence that contains an error in usage, punctuation, or grammar. If no errors are found, choose the last option.

a. Seeing his daughter for the first time made John cry.
b. There parents grounded Bill and Ben for a week.
c. The house was not damaged in the storm, but the yard was torn up.
d. No mistake.

5. Identify the sentence that contains an error in usage, punctuation, or grammar. If no errors are found, choose the last option.

a. Lesley's father doesn't understand the internet very well.
b. The boys were late getting to school because their car broke down.
c. We worked on the project for day's and still got a bad grade.
d. No mistake.

6. Identify the sentence that contains an error in usage, punctuation, or grammar. If no errors are found, choose the last option.

a. Bill passed his driving test on the first try.
b. My mother always did the grocery shopping and washed the dishes after dinner.
c. Amelia's punishment for being a bad girl was to go to bed with no dessert.
d. No mistake.

7. Identify the sentence that contains an error in usage, punctuation, or grammar. If no errors are found, choose the last option.

a. Ali drove across the country all by herself last summer.
b. The three textbooks you need is all in the bookstore.
c. My computer crashed last night.
d. No mistake.

8. Identify the sentence that contains an error in usage, punctuation, or grammar. If no errors are found, choose the last option.

a. The party was cancelled because of the rain.
b. My house is built on seven acres of land.
c. We went with them to the fair last year, but their not going this year.
d. No mistake.

9. Identify the sentence that contains an error in usage, punctuation, or grammar. If no errors are found, choose the last option.

a. My daughter was born with a full head of hair.
b. His car broke down for the fifth time this month.
c. Bruce Springsteen is often thought of as one of Americas' greatest songwriters.
d. No mistake.

10. Identify the sentence that contains an error in usage, punctuation, or grammar. If no errors are found, choose the last option.

a. Rocky always told people he was named after the famous movie character.
b. Alice's favorite way to relieve her stress is to go shopping at the mall.
c. Robin struggles with math, but she is very good at science.
d. No mistake.

11. Identify the sentence that contains an error in usage, punctuation, or grammar. If no errors are found, choose the last option.

a. She ate two.
b. The thief broke into the house through the basement window.
c. My grandmother sold her house and moved to Florida.
d. No mistake.

12. Identify the sentence that contains an error in usage, punctuation, or grammar. If no errors are found, choose the last option.

a. George Washington, and Abraham Lincoln are our two most famous leaders.
b. The President of the United States is thought of as the leader of the free world.
c. I went to a movie last week, but I didn't like it.
d. No mistake.

13. Identify the sentence that contains an error in usage, punctuation, or grammar. If no errors are found, choose the last option.

a. The US Constitution declares that all men are created equal.
b. My father graduated from college at the top of his class.
c. When I was in school, the Principal was a mean old woman.
d. No mistake.

14. Identify the sentence that contains an error in usage, punctuation, or grammar. If no errors are found, choose the last option.

a. The last house on my street was spooky old and creepy.
b. Jackie's mother always taught him that there were no such things as ghosts.
c. The hardware store closed ten minutes after I got there.
d. No mistake.

15. Identify the sentence that contains an error in usage, punctuation, or grammar. If no errors are found, choose the last option.

a. My sister loves cheese, but I hate it.
b. What town did your parent's grow up in?
c. There are three hundred sixty-five days in a year.
d. No mistake.

16. Identify the sentence that contains an error in usage, punctuation, or grammar. If no errors are found, choose the last option.

a. When Sam was growing up, his family had very little money.
b. The letter stated that my application had been denied, which was written on formal letterhead.
c. Babe Ruth is one of the most recognized names in American sports.
d. No mistake.

17. Identify the sentence that contains an error in usage, punctuation, or grammar. If no errors are found, choose the last option.

a. Bill was very nervous the first day of class; he had never been a teacher before.
b. The yellow house across the street is much older than ours.
c. When my brother said he was going to the movies, I said I wanted to go to.
d. No mistake.

18. Identify the sentence that contains an error in usage, punctuation, or grammar. If no errors are found, choose the last option.

a. My parents didn't let me watch television when I was growing up.
b. The movie was totally sold out; which stinks.
c. It took me three weeks to write my term paper.
d. No mistake.

19. Identify the sentence that contains an error in usage, punctuation, or grammar. If no errors are found, choose the last option.

a. The championship game was very exciting.
b. If I come to work early tomorrow, may I leave early as well?
c. The test had four kinds of questions: true or false, multiple choice, fill in the blank, and matching.
d. No mistake.

20. Identify the sentence that contains an error in usage, punctuation, or grammar. If no errors are found, choose the last option.

a. I can always tell when Jimmy is coming to get me because his car is so loud.
b. Steve loved playing football, baseball, and loved to run.
c. There are not enough hours in the day for me to get all my work done.
d. No mistake.

21. Identify the sentence that contains an error in usage, punctuation, or grammar. If no errors are found, choose the last option.

a. Blogging has become a very popular form of communication in the future.
b. Richard Pryor and George Carlin were very controversial in their time.
c. What day of the week is the party scheduled for?
d. No mistake.

22. Identify the sentence that contains an error in usage, punctuation, or grammar. If no errors are found, choose the last option.

a. Most people think John was the most talented of the Beatles, but I think it was Paul.
b. I failed the test three times before I finally passed it.
c. War is always a controversial issue.
d. No mistake.

23. Identify the sentence that contains an error in usage, punctuation, or grammar. If no errors are found, choose the last option.

a. "A mile isn't very far to run." said Steve.
b. I learned to ride horses when I was younger.
c. My grandmother goes to bed very early.
d. No mistake.

24. Identify the sentence that contains an error in usage, punctuation, or grammar. If no errors are found, choose the last option.

a. Answering three essay questions was very difficult.
b. Principal Walters and governor Jones had a debate on television.
c. I like cheese and I like macaroni, but I don't like macaroni and cheese.
d. No mistake.

25. Identify the sentence that contains an error in usage, punctuation, or grammar. If no errors are found, choose the last option.

a. His last business went bankrupt, so he's having a hard time getting a loan.
b. Peyton loved the sweater her grandmother bought her.
c. It's very comforting to know that we have such good insurance.
d. No mistake.

26. Identify the sentence that contains an error in usage, punctuation, or grammar. If no errors are found, choose the last option.

a. Did you like the movie or the book better?
b. Frank was sure he would never understand fractions.
c. Joan forgot to turn her headlights off, so her car battery ran out.
d. No mistake.

27. Identify the sentence that contains an error in usage, punctuation, or grammar. If no errors are found, choose the last option.

a. When I was in high school, I loved heavy metal music.
b. When Sue went to the mall and bought shoes she also bought a dress and some sandals.
c. Getting into college was much harder than Marc expected it to be.
d. No mistake.

28. Identify the sentence that contains an error in usage, punctuation, or grammar. If no errors are found, choose the last option.

a. Randall were very nervous on his wedding day.
b. The band played the fight song as the team took the court.
c. I don't believe in the death penalty, no matter what the crime was.
d. No mistake.

29. Identify the sentence that contains an error in usage, punctuation, or grammar. If no errors are found, choose the last option.

a. The team won the state championship three years in a row.
b. Ben fell asleep on the bus and missed his stop.
c. Two wrongs don't not make a right.
d. No mistake.

30. Identify the sentence that contains an error in usage, punctuation, or grammar. If no errors are found, choose the last option.

a. If Scott and Lucy got married, they would be very happy.
b. I went to the store, but I forgot to buy bread
c. John is afraid of snakes, dogs, and spiders.
d. No mistake.

31. Identify the sentence that contains an error in usage, punctuation, or grammar. If no errors are found, choose the last option.

a. George gets tired very easily especially when he is doing hard work.
b. The house burned down, but no one was hurt.
c. My daughter loves to watch I Love Lucy on television.
d. No mistake.

32. Identify the sentence that contains an error in usage, punctuation, or grammar. If no errors are found, choose the last option.

a. Lesley liked to take showers at night rather than in the morning.
b. The grocery store was completely sold out of watermelon.
c. By the time he finished the test, Jack was exhausted.
d. No mistake.

33. Identify the sentence that contains an error in usage, punctuation, or grammar. If no errors are found, choose the last option.

a. I went to the hospital to talk to the doctor on Grant Street.
b. King Tut is the most famous of the ancient Egyptian rulers.
c. Jackie Robinson broke baseball's color barrier.
d. No mistake.

34. Identify the sentence that contains an error in usage, punctuation, or grammar. If no errors are found, choose the last option.

a. I was hoping I did well enough on the test to pass.
b. My father was always very strict but fair.
c. Susan asked the instructor how long the essay had to be, but he wouldn't tell her.
d. No mistake.

35. Identify the sentence that contains an error in usage, punctuation or grammar. If no errors are found, choose the last option.

a. Adam Sandler is my favorite comedian.
b. My sister Julie always got Jerry Lewis and Jerry Lee Lewis confused.
c. I always enjoyed reading, writing, and to sing a song.
d. No mistake.

36. Identify the sentence that contains an error in usage, punctuation, or grammar. If no errors are found, choose the last option.

a. There is nothing Margie likes better than a good deep dish pizza.
b. Her favorite subject in school was english.
c. Will you be joining us for the trip to Miami?
d. No mistake.

37. Identify the sentence that contains an error in usage, punctuation, or grammar. If no errors are found, choose the last option.

a. I love movies, and television, but I like reading better.
b. Michael Jackson was one of the most famous musical artists of all time.
c. The temperature was so hot, it was almost impossible to go outside.
d. No mistake.

38. Identify the sentence that contains an error in usage, punctuation, or grammar. If no errors are found, choose the last option.

a. I may drink beer sometimes, but I will never drink wine.
b. He will go to the game, but didn't stay long.
c. We followed the road signs, but should've followed the map.
d. No mistake.

39. Identify the sentence that contains an error in usage, punctuation, or grammar. If no errors are found, choose the last option.

a. I was quite scared about the results of my blood tests.
b. If you give the dog it's bone, it might stop begging for food.
c. What time does Mary usually get home from work?
d. No mistake.

40. Select the sentence with an error in spelling. If no errors are found, choose the last option.

a. I wasn't home the night my brother came home from college.
b. Most teachers, police officers, and fire fighters are underpaid.
c. I've always had trouble with commas, semicolons, and hyphens.
d. No mistake.

41. Select the sentence with an error in spelling. If no errors are found, choose the last option.

a. I hated going to school when I was younger.
b. I was lazie and didn't like doing the work.
c. As I got older, I realized that I should have worked harder.
d. No mistake.

42. Select the sentence with an error in spelling. If no errors are found, choose the last option.

a. My father was a star athlete in college.
b. I didn't like sports.
c. My father may have been better at sports, but I got better grades.
d. No mistake.

43. Select the sentence with an error in spelling. If no errors are found, choose the last option.

a. When I wreked my car, I was worried it was totaled.
b. The mechanic said he could fix it.
c. Even though it was very expensive, I was very relieved.
d. No mistake.

44. Select the sentence with an error in spelling. If no errors are found, choose the last option.

a. The summer was very hot this year.
b. I don't like the heat, so I was looking forward to winter.
c. When winter came, it was so cold that I wished it was summer again.
d. No mistake.

45. Select the sentence with an error in spelling. If no errors are found, choose the last option.

a. My computer stopped working in the middle of writing my essay.
b. I was sure I had lost everything.
c. The tecnician from computer support got it working again and saved my essay.
d. No mistake.

46. Select the sentence with an error in spelling. If no errors are found, choose the last option.

a. My first aparpment was the smallest place I'd ever seen.
b. I couldn't believe I was paying so much for so little.
c. When I finally moved out, I was so happy.
d. No mistake.

47. Select the sentence with an error in spelling. If no errors are found, choose the last option.

a. My mother ran four miles every day.
b. She was always in great shape.
c. When I realized how overwait I was, I started running with her.
d. No mistake.

48. Select the sentence with an error in spelling. If no errors are found, choose the last option.

a. Julie believed her house was haunted.
b. She said their were ghosts in the attic.
c. All of her friends thought she was crazy.
d. No mistake.

49. Select the sentence with an error in spelling. If no errors are found, choose the last option.

a. Television is one of the greatest inventions of all time.
b. Before the Internet came along, television was what brought the world together.
c. Even now, television links people together.
d. No mistake.

50. Select the sentence with an error in spelling. If no errors are found, choose the last option.

a. When I graduated from college, I couldn't find a job.
b. I thought someone would hire me right away.
c. Eventually, I found a job, but it wasn't what I'd accepted.
d. No mistake.

51. Where should the following sentence be placed in the paragraph below?

The iPad is the most popular of the new tablet computers.

1.) Experts predict that tablet computers will outsell desktop computers by 2015. 2.) Tablet computers have been gaining in popularity over the last year or so. 3.) Even the iPad though doesn't sell as well as most laptop or desktop computers. 4.) If tablet computers are going to outsell desktops, they will have to become much more popular.

a. After sentence 1
b. After sentence 2
c. After sentence 3
d. After sentence 4

52. Where should the following sentence be placed in the paragraph below?

His most famous novel is probably *The Adventures of Huckleberry Finn*.

1.) Mark Twain was one of America's greatest writers. 2.) Twain stopped writing the book for several years because he didn't know where the story would go. 3.) Most readers can tell the spot where he stopped, because the book is much different after that. 4.) The entire tone of the novel is different and it becomes a much darker story.

a. After sentence 1
b. After sentence 2
c. After sentence 3
d. After sentence 4

53. Writing, doing yoga, and _______ were her favorite activities.

a. playing volleyball
b. doing volleyball
c. making volleyball
d. volleyballing

54. Every kid in the neighborhood has _____ own bicycle.

a. its
b. their
c. our
d. her

55. Choose the word or words that best fill the blank.

A team of scientists _______ studying a new species of frog never found before.

a. is
b. are
c. were
d. have

56. Consider the following sentence:

Dr. Anderson strolled past the nurses, examining a bottle of pills.

Select the best version of the sentence.

a. NO CHANGE
b. Dr. Anderson strolled past the nurses examining a bottle of pills.
c. Dr. Anderson strolled past, the nurses examining a bottle of pills.
d. Examining a bottle of pills, Dr. Anderson strolled past the nurses.

57. Consider the following sentence:

Mr. King, <u>an individual of considerable influence, created a personal fortune and gave back to the community.</u>

Select the best version of the underlined portion.

a. NO CHANGE
b. an individual of considerable influence, he created a personal fortune and gave back
c. an individual of considerable influence created a personal fortune and gave back
d. an individual of considerable influence, created a personal fortune and gave it back

58. Consider the following sentence:

She is the person whose opinion matters the most.

Select the best version of the sentence.

a. NO CHANGE
b. She is the person to whom her opinion matters the most.
c. She is the person her opinion matters the most.
d. She is the person for whom her opinion matters the most.

59. Which sentence does not belong in the following paragraph?

1.) The New York Yankees have won more World Series championships than any other team in baseball. 2.) They have a total of twenty-seven titles. 3.) They have had some of the most famous players in history, including Babe Ruth and Mickey Mantle. 4.) The Yankees won the World Series four consecutive times from 1936 to 1939. 5.) They repeated the feat from 1949 to 1953. 6.) The Yankees won their twenty-seventh World Series title in 2009.

a. Sentence 2
b. Sentence 3
c. Sentence 4
d. Sentence 5

60. Which sentence does not belong in the following paragraph?

1.) Climate change is a very controversial topic. 2.) Many experts claim that our planet's climate is changing. 3.) These experts believe that climate change is why we experience hotter summers and warmer winters. 4.) Other experts argue that the changes in temperature are normal. 5.) Last summer, it was so hot I had to install three air conditioners in my home. 6.) Both sides have a great deal of scientific evidence to back up their claims.

a. Sentence 2
b. Sentence 3
c. Sentence 4
d. Sentence 5

Verbal Skills

1. Secede means the *opposite* of:

a. Accessible
b. Recall
c. Merge
d. Bail

2. Taciturn is to reserved as loquacious is to:

a. Definitive
b. Talkative
c. Refined
d. Sanguine

3. Object most nearly means:

a. Disagree
b. State
c. Concur
d. Relate

4. University Press received more submissions than Institutes Press. Institutes Press received fewer submissions than Academy Press. Academy Press received more submissions than University Press. If the first two statements are true, then the third is:

a. True
b. False
c. Unknown
d. Redundant

5. Decade is to 10 as millennium is to:

a. 100
b. 10,000
c. 1,000
d. 1,000,000

6. Driver is to truck as:

a. Horse is to rider
b. Hiker is to trail
c. Waiter is to restaurant
d. Engineer is to train

7. Ellie was born one minute after Dean. Dean was born before Rob. Rob was born after Ellie. If the first two statements are true, then the third is:

a. True
b. False
c. Unknown
d. A contradiction

8. Susceptible most nearly means:

a. Acceptable
b. Vulnerable
c. Available
d. Capable

9. Which word does NOT belong with the others?

a. Novel
b. Short story
c. Autobiography
d. Play

10. Denny has more trading cards than Barry. Barry has fewer cards than Steve. Steve has more than Denny. If the first two sentences are true, then the third one is:

a. True
b. False
c. Uncertain

11. Soiled most nearly means:

a. Dirty
b. Sullen
c. Sultry
d. Dainty

12. Flagrant means the *opposite* of:

a. Blatant
b. Obvious
c. Clear
d. Obscure

13. Bare most nearly means:

a. Concealed
b. Uniformed
c. Revealed
d. Dressed

14. Kevin watched fewer television shows than Allen. John watched more television shows than Allen. John watched the greatest amount of television shows of the three. If the first two statements are true, then the third is:

a. True
b. False
c. Unknown
d. A contradiction

15. Lucid means the *opposite* of:

a. Clear
b. Confused
c. Sound
d. Logical

16. Samuel invented more patents than his brother James. Horace had twice as many patents as James. Samuel and Horace had the same number of patents. If the first two statements are true, then the third is:

a. True
b. False
c. Unknown
d. Unimportant

17. Which word does NOT belong with the others?

a. Jupiter
b. Moon
c. Earth
d. Saturn

18. Which word does NOT belong with the others?

a. Copper
b. Gold
c. Aluminum
d. Sulfur

19. Underdog is to audacious as conspirator is to:

a. Altruistic
b. Elusive
c. Illegible
d. Passive

20. Which word does NOT belong with the others?

a. Counselor
b. Nurse
c. Lawyer
d. Novelist

21. **Opulent most nearly means:**
    a. Vivacious
    b. Affluent
    c. Virulent
    d. Impoverished

22. **Discord is the *opposite* of:**
    a. Harmony
    b. Strife
    c. Attrition
    d. Angst

23. **Pinnacle is the *opposite* of:**
    a. Ornate
    b. Null
    c. Apex
    d. Base

24. **Which word does NOT belong with the others?**
    a. Sleet
    b. Precipitation
    c. Snow
    d. Rain

25. **Inanimate most nearly means:**
    a. Active
    b. Cartoon
    c. Motionless
    d. Animal

26. **Valuable means the *opposite* of:**
    a. Precious
    b. Costly
    c. Worthless
    d. Priceless

27. **Compact means the *opposite* of:**
    a. Dense
    b. Squashed
    c. Compressed
    d. Loose

28. **Complacent most nearly means:**
    a. Cautious
    b. Astute
    c. Nonchalant
    d. Chivalrous

29. Outspoken most nearly means:

a. Demure
b. Introverted
c. Candid
d. Precise

30. Impartial most nearly means:

a. Dignified
b. Biased
c. Deceptive
d. Equitable

31. John is tall. John is a basketball player for his high school team. All basketball players on John's high school team are tall. If the first two statements are true, then the third statement is:

a. True
b. False
c. Unknown

32. Homage most nearly means:

a. Household
b. Image
c. Mockery
d. Tribute

33. Pandemonium most nearly means:

a. Chaos
b. Animal
c. Monetary
d. Masculine

34. Generous most nearly means:

a. Giving
b. Truthful
c. Selfish
d. Harsh

35. Aptitude most nearly means:

a. Talent
b. Test
c. Height
d. Disposition

36. Residence most nearly means:

a. Home
b. Area
c. Plan
d. Resist

37. Dictate most nearly means:

a. Allow
b. Tell
c. Prevent
d. Ask

38. Jamie sold fewer ice cream cones than Emily during their shift at the ice cream shop. Brianna sold double the amount of ice cream cones as Emily. Brianna sold fewer ice cream cones than Jamie. If the first two statements are true, then the third statement is:

a. True
b. False
c. Unknown

39. Bunch is to flowers as:

a. Bale is to hay
b. Walnut is to shell
c. Cake is to party
d. Butterfly is to wing

40. Which word does NOT belong with the others?

a. Footballs
b. Basketballs
c. Hockey pucks
d. Sporting gear

41. Which word does NOT belong with the others?

a. Restaurant
b. Airport
c. Cape Cod
d. Hotel

42. Berate most nearly means:

a. Payment
b. Scale
c. Time
d. Scold

43. Scissors is to haircut as tractor is to:

a. Farmer
b. Harvest
c. Soil
d. Corn fields

44. Refute most nearly means:

a. Disprove
b. Disillusion
c. Distinguish
d. Disappoint

45. Endearment most nearly means:

a. Suspicion
b. Affection
c. Venison
d. Imprisonment

46. Index is to book as elegy is to:

a. Artifact
b. Audition
c. Equinox
d. Funeral

47. Arithmetic operations are to algebra as organisms are to:

a. Chemistry
b. Physics
c. Psychology
d. Biology

48. Allison likes foxes more than beetles. Kelsey likes sheep more than caterpillars. Both Allison and Kelsey like mammals more than insects. If the first two statements are true, then the third statement is:

a. True
b. False
c. Unknown

49. Aural most nearly means:

a. Hearing
b. Language
c. Circular
d. Drill

50. Paltry most nearly means:

a. Cheap
b. Valuable
c. Peaceful
d. Plenty

51. Which word does NOT belong with the others?

a. Guitar
b. Drummer
c. Saxophone
d. Piano

52. Pallid most nearly means:

a. Healthy
b. Sickly
c. Rosy
d. Deep

53. Grapes are to wine as:

a. Catsup is to French fries
b. Coffee is to cup
c. Chair is to table
d. Wheat is to bread

54. Jog is to marathon as hypothesis is to:

a. Discovery
b. Forgery
c. Irate
d. Surreal

55. Which word does NOT belong with the others?

a. Painter
b. Artist
c. Musician
d. Dancer

56. Year is to month as foot is to:

a. Inch
b. Yard
c. Meter
d. Mile

57. Antipathy is to sympathy as convivial is to:

a. Avarice
b. Gloomy
c. Harmonious
d. Sociable

58. Arrive is to enter as acquiesce is to:

a. Determine
b. Accede
c. Encounter
d. Scorn

59. Foster most nearly means:

a. Nurture
b. Woods
c. Home
d. Retain

60. Active means the *opposite* of:

a. Electrical
b. Moving
c. Inert
d. Positive

Quantitative Skills

1. Which of the following is correct?

a. $\frac{4}{7} = \frac{12}{21}$
b. $\frac{3}{4} = \frac{12}{20}$
c. $\frac{5}{8} = \frac{15}{32}$
d. $\frac{7}{9} = \frac{28}{45}$

2. Which of the following is the largest number?

a. 0.003
b. 0.300
c. 0.1
d. 0.20

3. Doug drives without backtracking from his apartment to a campsite in another state. His trip requires him to travel at various speeds, and at one point he gets stuck in traffic. After two hours, he is halfway to his destination. After four hours, he is two-thirds of the way there. Which of the following could represent the fraction of his travel distance he has covered after three hours?

a. $\frac{2}{5}$
b. $\frac{3}{5}$
c. $\frac{3}{4}$
d. $\frac{4}{5}$

4. You want to rent a lawn mower. The cost is $12 per day plus a one-time registration fee of $20. If your budget allows you to spend no more than $220 on this rental, how many whole days can you rent the lawn mower?

a. 20 days
b. 18 days
c. 17 days
d. 16 days

5. An equilateral triangle has sides of length 10 inches, and a square has sides of length 5 inches. How do the perimeters of the triangle and the square compare?

a. The perimeter of the triangle is twice as long as that of the square.
b. The perimeter of the square is longer than that of the triangle.
c. The triangle and the square have the same perimeter.
d. The perimeter of the triangle is longer than that of the square but is less than twice as long.

6. How do the perimeters of pentagon *A* and pentagon *B* compare? All measurements are in centimeters (cm).

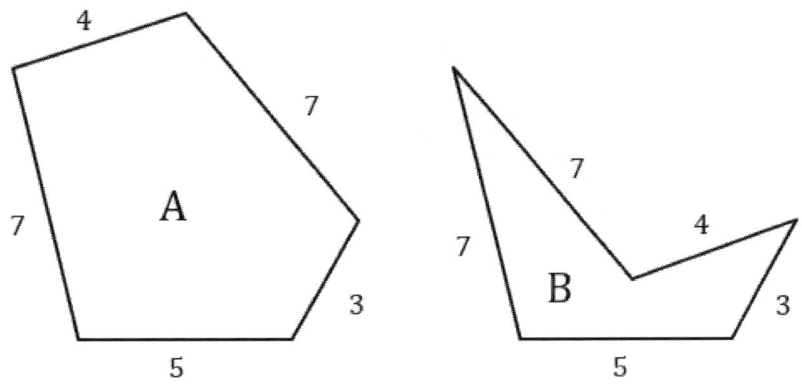

a. The perimeter of pentagon *A* is shorter than that of pentagon *B*.
b. The perimeter of pentagon *A* is the same as that of pentagon *B*.
c. The perimeter of pentagon *A* is more than twice that of pentagon *B*.
d. The perimeter of pentagon *A* is longer than that of pentagon *B* but less than twice that of pentagon *B*.

7. Look for patterns along rows and/or columns to determine the unknown value of x.

3	**15**	**10**
8	**40**	**35**
6	**30**	x

a. 25
b. 30
c. 40
d. 45

8. Which of the following statements correctly compares the decimal numbers 0.24, 0.237, and 0.2366?

a. $0.2366 < 0.24 < 0.237$
b. $0.24 < 0.237 < 0.2366$
c. $0.237 < 0.2366 < 0.24$
d. $0.2366 < 0.237 < 0.24$

9. Which of the following correctly compares the given rational numbers?

a. $0.2 > 0.0499 > 0.007$
b. $0 < -2 < 7$
c. $\frac{1}{5} > \frac{1}{4} > \frac{1}{3}$
d. $-1 < -4 < -10$

10. Which of the following numbers is the smallest?

a. 2^8
b. 3^3
c. 16^1
d. 24

11. Use the rule $2x + 0.5$ to determine the missing term for y in the sequence.

x	0	1	2	3
y	0.5	2.5	4.5	

a. 5.5
b. 6
c. 6.5
d. 7

12. Davis and Christopher are running a race. They agree that Davis is a faster runner, so they give Christopher a 100-foot head start. Suppose both runners start at the same time. Davis runs at a steady 9.4 feet per second, and Christopher runs at a steady 8.6 feet per second. How long does it take Davis to catch up to Christopher?

a. 125 seconds
b. 123 seconds
c. 118 seconds
d. Davis does not catch up to Christopher.

13. What is the 10th term in the sequence?

96, 48, 24, 12...

a. 0.1875
b. 0.857
c. 1.0878
d. 1.887

14. Which of the following can be divided by 3, with no remainder?

a. 46
b. 555
c. 2,018
d. 8,912

15. 5 people are in a race. Racer A finishes before Racer B, but behind Racer C. Racer D finished before Racer E, but behind Racer B. What was the finishing race order from first to last?

a. C, A, E, D, B
b. C, A, B, E, D
c. C, A, B, D, E
d. D, C, A, B, E

16. These polygons are similar (that is, corresponding angles have equal measure and corresponding sides have proportional lengths) and their bases have lengths (in meters) as marked.

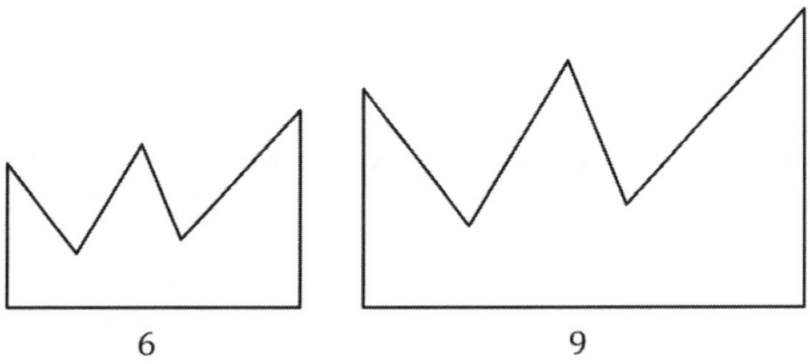

If the polygon on the left (the smaller polygon) has a perimeter of 22 meters, what is the perimeter of the polygon on the right (the larger polygon)?

a. 25 meters
b. 33 meters
c. 43 meters
d. 44 meters

17. What does the variable *d* represent in the following formula?

$$a_n = a_1 + (n - 1)d$$

a. Common denominator
b. Common ratio
c. nth term
d. Common difference

18. A right triangle has a hypotenuse of length 25 and a leg of length 24.

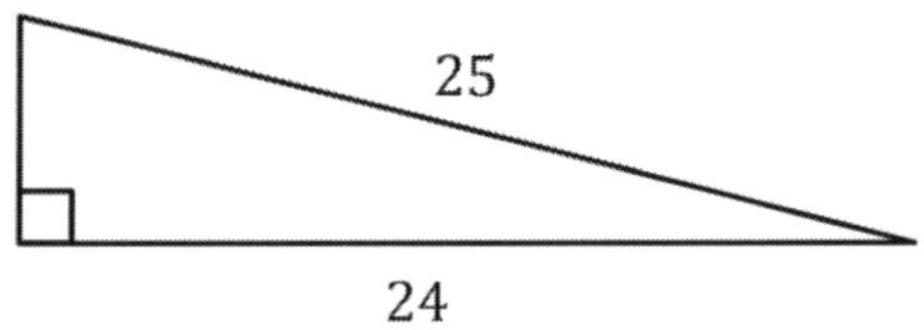

How long is the hypotenuse compared to the other leg of the triangle?

a. The hypotenuse is shorter than the other leg.
b. The hypotenuse is longer than the other leg, but less than twice as long.
c. The hypotenuse is between 2 and 3 times as long as the other leg.
d. The hypotenuse is more than 3 times as long as the other leg.

19. Assume a runner runs at a constant rate without getting tired or slowing down. Which race would take the least amount of time to finish: the 4 × 100 meter relay race, the 200-meter race, or the 5-kilometer race?

a. 4 × 100 relay race
b. 200-meter race
c. 5-kilometer race
d. All three races should take the same amount of time.

20. A triangle has angles of 23° and 101°, and an unknown angle of x°. A quadrilateral has angles of 90°, 123°, and 93°, and an unknown angle of y°. How do x and y compare?

a. $y > 2x$
b. $y < x < 2y$
c. $x > 2y$
d. $x < y < 2x$

21. What number should fill in the blank for the sequence?

15.5, 15.9, 16.3, ____, 17.1, 17.5...

a. 16.3
b. 16.5
c. 16.7
d. 16.9

22. Order these lengths from shortest to longest: 75 inches, 2 yards, and 7 feet.

a. 2 yards, 7 feet, 75 inches
b. 75 inches, 2 yards, 7 feet
c. 7 feet, 75 inches, 2 yards
d. 2 yards, 75 inches, 7 feet

23. Find the next term in the sequence.

$$-\frac{1}{2}, -\frac{2}{3}, -\frac{5}{6}, \_\_$$

a. $-\frac{7}{6}$
b. -1
c. $-\frac{4}{6}$
d. 1

24. Which of the following inequalities is true?

a. $\frac{7}{8} < \frac{6}{7}$
b. $\frac{9}{10} > \frac{11}{12}$
c. $\frac{2}{3} > \frac{9}{13}$
d. $\frac{1}{4} < \frac{2}{7}$

25. A triangle has sides of length 4 feet and 9 feet. Which statement is necessarily true about the third side of the triangle?

a. The third side is longer than 5 feet and shorter than 13 feet.
b. The third side is longer than 9 feet.
c. The third side is shorter than 9 feet.
d. There is no restriction on the possible length of the third side.

26. What is the 15th term in the sequence?

17, 19, 21, 23...

a. 38
b. 40
c. 45
d. 49

27. A university has a Music Appreciation class with 108 students, a Databases class with 120 students, a German Literature class with 28 students, and a Calculus class 42 students. If sophomores make up $\frac{1}{6}$ of the Music Appreciation students, $\frac{3}{20}$ of the Databases students, $\frac{3}{4}$ of the German Literature students, and $\frac{3}{7}$ of the Calculus students, which class has the most sophomores?

a. Music Appreciation
b. Databases
c. German Literature
d. Calculus

28. Which of the following numbers is greatest?

a. 0.0236
b. 0.236
c. 0.0339
d. 0.099

29. Use the rule $0.4x + 3$ to determine the missing term for y in the sequence.

x	0	1	2	3
y		3.4	3.8	4.2

a. 3.2
b. 3.1
c. 3.0
d. 2.8

30. Which of the following is an example of a geometric sequence?

a. 1, 8, 15, 22...
b. 20, 17, 14, 11...
c. 1, 2, 3, 4...
d. 324, 108, 36, 12...

31. Josh and Peter run laps after school each day. For every 3 laps that Josh runs, Peter runs 5 laps. If Josh runs 18 laps, how many will Peter run?

a. 26
b. 27
c. 30
d. 32

32. Calculate the 10th term in the sequence below.

3, 6, 12, 24...

a. 106
b. 536
c. 1,536
d. 15,360

33. Which choice correctly shows the nth term formula for arithmetic sequences?

a. $a_n = a_1 r^{n-1}$
b. $a_n = a_1 r^{n+1}$
c. $a_n = a_1 + (n-1)d$
d. $a_n = a_1 + (n+1)d$

34. Use the rule $\frac{6x}{2}$ to determine the missing term for y in the sequence.

x	2	4	6	8
y	6		18	24

a. 10
b. 12
c. 12.5
d. 14

35. All the sequences listed below are either geometric or arithmetic, except one. Which sequence is neither geometric nor arithmetic?

a. 2, 10, 50, 250...
b. 7.5, 32.5, 57.5, 82.5...
c. 17, 15, 13, 11...
d. 2, 3, 5, 8...

36. Which of the following inequalities is correct?

a. $\frac{1}{3} < \frac{2}{7} < \frac{5}{12}$
b. $\frac{2}{7} < \frac{1}{3} < \frac{5}{12}$
c. $\frac{5}{12} < \frac{2}{7} < \frac{1}{3}$
d. $\frac{5}{12} < \frac{1}{3} < \frac{2}{7}$

37. What is the first term in a sequence that has a common difference of 4, and the 16th term is 91?

a. 21
b. 27
c. 31
d. 33

38. Drew has half of a pizza. He cuts his pizza into two equal shares, then he cuts each piece again in half. What fraction of a whole pizza is each piece?

a. $\frac{1}{2}$
b. $\frac{1}{4}$
c. $\frac{1}{8}$
d. $\frac{1}{6}$

39. Jose drinks 1 quart of juice. John drinks 1 pint of juice. Julie drinks $\frac{1}{2}$ gallon of juice. Who drank the most juice?

a. Jose
b. John
c. Julie
d. Jose, John, and Julie drank the same amount.

40. A triangle has three angles: angle *A*, angle *B*, and angle *C*. If angle *A* measures 64°, which one of the following statements is necessarily true? (Hint: The three angles of a triangle always add up to 180°.)

a. Angle *A* is the largest angle in the triangle.
b. Angle *A* is the smallest angle in the triangle.
c. Angle *A* is not the smallest angle in the triangle.
d. Angle *A* is not the largest angle in the triangle.

41. Cube *A* has edges that are 2 feet long, and cube *B* has edges that are 3 feet long. Which statement correctly describes their volumes?

a. The volume of cube *B* is less than twice the volume of cube *A*.
b. The volume of cube *B* is between 2 and 3 times the volume of cube *A*.
c. The volume of cube *B* is between 3 and 4 times the volume of cube *A*.
d. The volume of cube *B* is more than 4 times the volume of cube *A*.

42. What number is half of the product of 4, 5, and 6?

a. 40
b. 50
c. 60
d. 80

43. As the owner of a school supplies store, you sell calculators at a 25% markup. That is, the price you offer on each calculator is 25% higher than what you paid for it. One day you hold a special sale in which you advertise that every item in the store is 10% off the usual price. During the sale, what will a customer pay, before tax, to buy a calculator that cost you $80?

a. $66
b. $90
c. $92
d. $108

44. Lynn has twice as many apples as Adam. Together they have 12 apples. How many apples does Lynn have?

a. 6
b. 7
c. 8
d. 9

45. Which choice represents a geometric sequence?

a. 6, 3, 0, −3, −6…
b. 4, 8, 16, 32…
c. 5, 9, 13, 17…
d. 20, 17, 14, 11…

46. Find the smallest whole number x such that $\frac{x}{9} > \frac{7}{11}$.

a. $x = 7$
b. $x = 5$
c. $x = 6$
d. $x = 8$

47. Which number is three times the difference between 17 and 36?

a. 19
b. 38
c. 57
d. 60

48. Jane runs 300 meters on the treadmill in her first minute of exercise. The distance she runs decreases by 15% for each of the following 5 minutes. About how many meters did Jane run in the 4th minute of exercise?

a. 184
b. 205
c. 215
d. 225

49. The ratio of blueberries to strawberries in fruit bowl is 5 : 6. If there are 48 strawberries in the bowl, how many berries are there altogether?

a. 70
b. 77
c. 80
d. 88

50. We have a box (also known as a rectangular solid) and a square pyramid. The box has length 5 feet, width 4 feet, and height 3 feet. The pyramid has height 5 feet, and its square base has edges of length 6 feet. How do the volumes of the box and pyramid compare?

a. The box has a larger volume than the pyramid.
b. The box has the same volume as the pyramid.
c. The pyramid's volume is more than twice that of the box.
d. The pyramid has a volume that is larger than that of the box, but less than twice as large.

51. Each figure is cut into triangular pieces. How many pieces would a 10-sided figure contain?

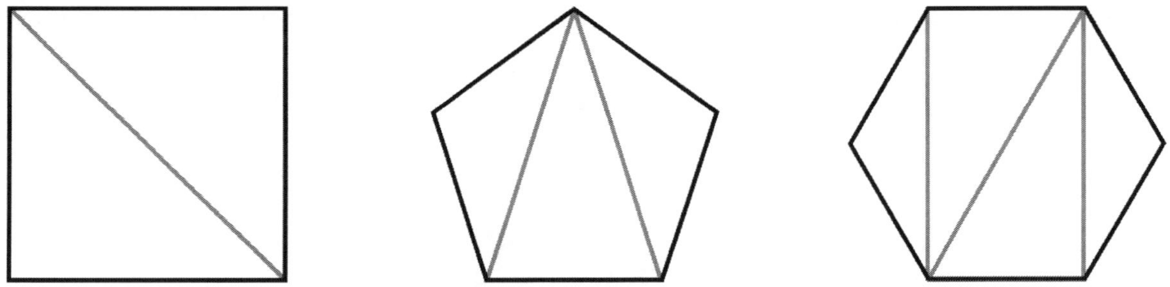

a. 7
b. 8
c. 10
d. 11

52. Point A has coordinates $(-2, -3)$. Point B has coordinates $(5, 4)$. Point C has coordinates $(1, 1)$. Which pair of points is farthest away from each other?

a. Points B and C
b. Points A and C
c. Points A and B
d. Two pairs of points are tied for being farthest away from each other.

Mathematics

1. Given the equation, $ax + b = c$, what is the value of x?

a. $\frac{c+b}{a}$
b. $\frac{ca}{b}$
c. $c - ba$
d. $\frac{c-b}{a}$

2. Evaluate the expression $2^3 + (4 + 1)$.

a. 9
b. 13
c. 15
d. 21

3. The 6th grade teachers at Washington Elementary School are doing a collaborative unit on cherry trees. Miss Wilson's math classes are making histograms summarizing the heights of black cherry trees located at a local fruit orchard. How many of the trees at this local orchard are 73 feet tall?

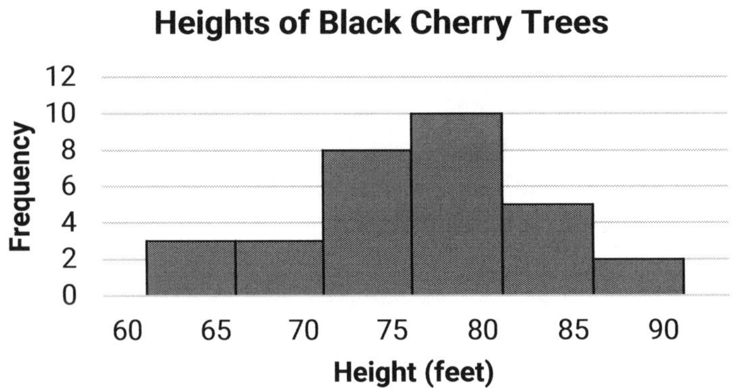

a. 8
b. 9
c. 17
d. That information cannot be obtained from this graph

4. Will needed his dinner to include at least 50 grams of protein, so he wanted to make sure he was eating enough chicken. He recalled that chicken has approximately 25 grams of protein in a 4-oz serving. He didn't have a scale that weighed ounces, but he had a 5-lb bag of flour that he planned to divide into equal portions to approximate the weight of chicken he needed, so that he could compare the weight of the flour to the chicken. Which of the following shows the calculation for the number of portions Will must divide the flour into?

a. $50 \times \frac{4}{25} \times \frac{1}{16} \times 5$
b. $25 \times 4 \times \frac{1}{16} \times \frac{1}{5}$
c. $1 \times 5 \times 16 \times \frac{25}{4} \times \frac{1}{50}$
d. $\frac{25}{4} \times \frac{16}{1} \times \frac{1}{5} \times 50$

5. What is the value of $894 + [(3)(12)]$?

a. 730
b. 930
c. 932
d. 945

6. Which of the following graphs does NOT represent a function?

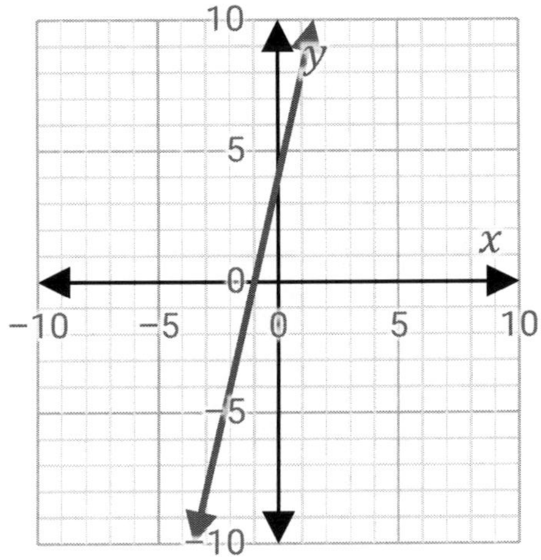

a.

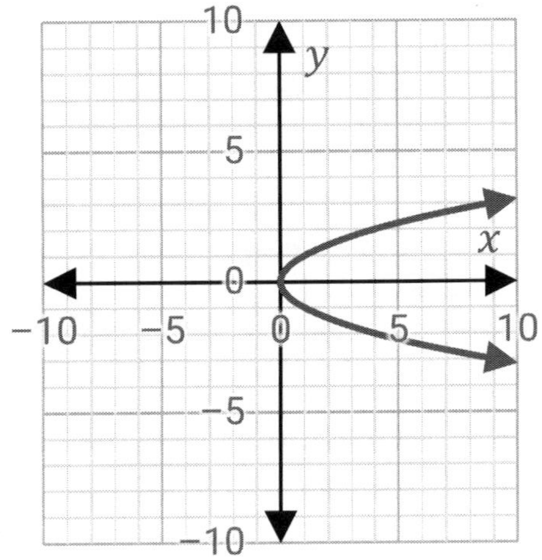

b.

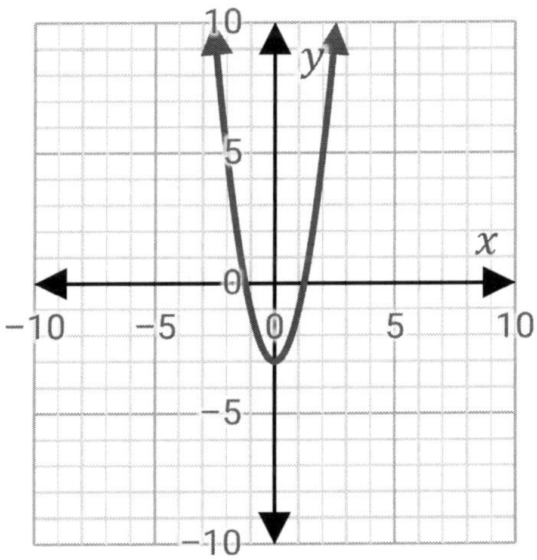

c.

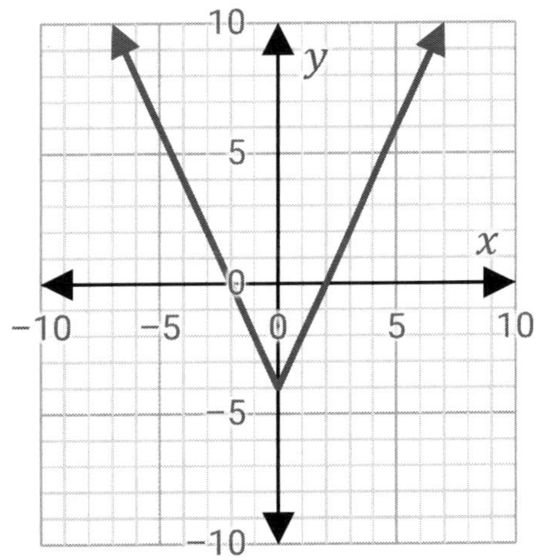

d.

7. A boy has a bag with 26 pieces of candy inside. He eats 8 pieces of candy, then divides the rest evenly between two friends. How many pieces of candy will each friend get?

a. 7
b. 9
c. 11
d. 13

8. Use the figure below to answer question.

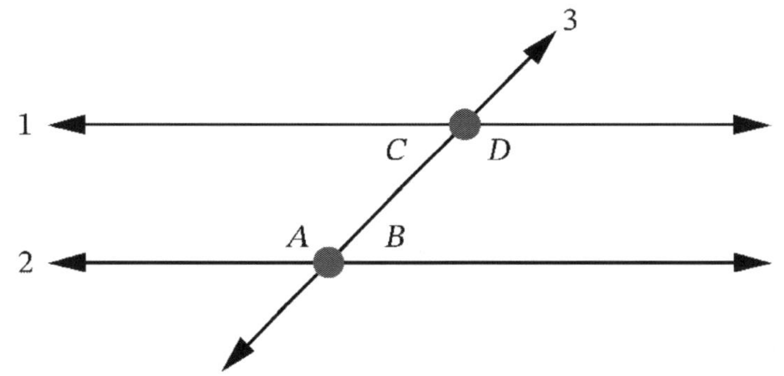

If $m\angle C = m\angle B$, which of the following statements is true about the figure above?

a. Lines 1 and 2 are parallel.
b. Lines 1 and 3 are parallel.
c. Lines 1 and 2 intersect.
d. Lines 1 and 3 are coincident.

9. Which of the following numbers is equal to 3^0?

a. 0
b. 1
c. 3
d. The number is not defined

10. The figure shows an irregular quadrilateral and the lengths of its sides. Which of the following expressions best represents the perimeter of the quadrilateral?

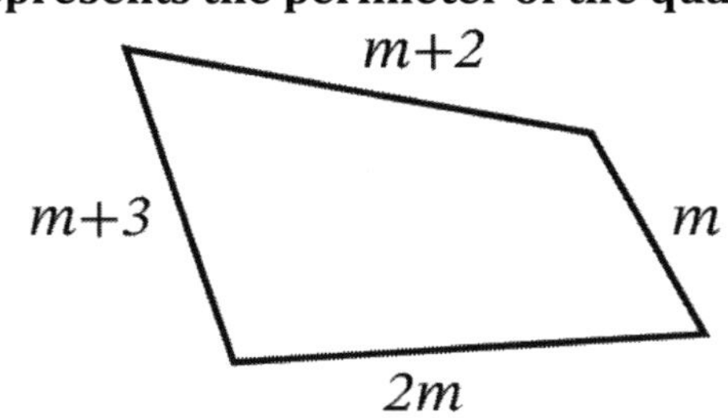

a. $m^4 + 5$
b. $2m^4 + 5$
c. $4m + 5$
d. $5m + 5$

11. A man's lawn grass is 3 inches high. He mows the lawn and cuts off 30% of its height. How tall will the grass be after the lawn is mowed?

a. 0.9 inches
b. 2.1 inches
c. 2.7 inches
d. 2.9 inches

12. A shirt is marked down by 25% and placed on a clearance rack, on which is posted a sign reading, "Take an extra 30% off already reduced merchandise." What fraction of the original price is the final sale price of the shirt?

a. $\frac{9}{20}$
b. $\frac{11}{20}$
c. $\frac{21}{40}$
d. $\frac{7}{10}$

13. What is $(4 + 6)^3$?

a. 10
b. 100
c. 1,000
d. 10,000

14. The sum of 34 and what number is equal to the product of 7 and 6?

a. 1
b. 4
c. 8
d. 12

15. In a town of 35,638 people, about a quarter of the population is under the age of 35. Of those, just over a third attend local K–12 schools. If the number of students in each grade is about the same, how many fourth graders likely reside in the town?

a. Fewer than 100
b. Between 200 and 300
c. Between 300 and 400
d. More than 400

16. Which of the following represents the net of a tetrahedron?

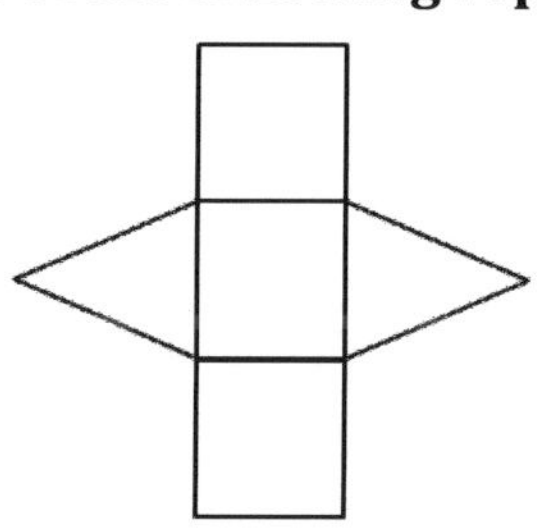
a.

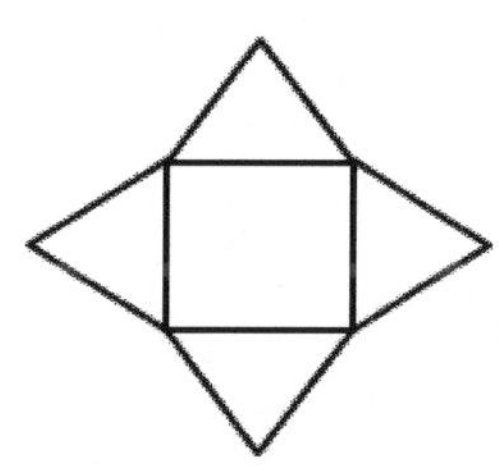
b.

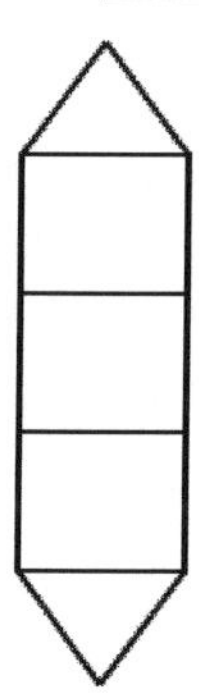
c.

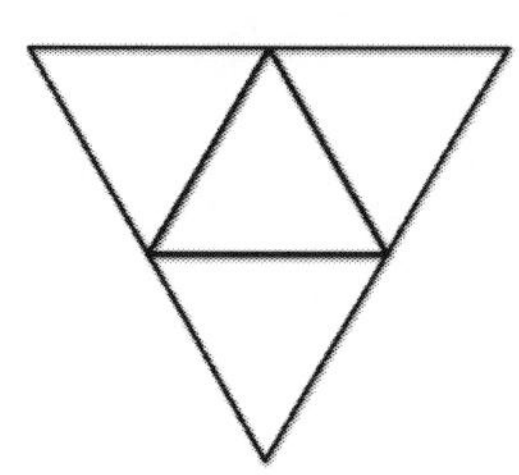
d.

17. Bruce works a part-time job every Monday through Wednesday. He is not allowed to work more than 12 hours in a week. One week he works 2 hours and 47 minutes on Monday and 4 hours and 56 minutes on Tuesday. What is the most time that he is allowed to work on Wednesday?

a. 4 hours and 17 minutes
b. 4 hours and 57 minutes
c. 5 hours and 17 minutes
d. 7 hours and 43 minutes

18. How many kilograms are equivalent to 58.6 grams?

a. 58,600 kg
b. 5,860 kg
c. 0.586 kg
d. 0.0586 kg

19. A woman has $450 in a bank account. She earns 5% interest on her end-of-month balance. How much interest will she earn for the month?

a. $5.00
b. $22.50
c. $427.50
d. $472.50

20. What is a true statement about the circles below?

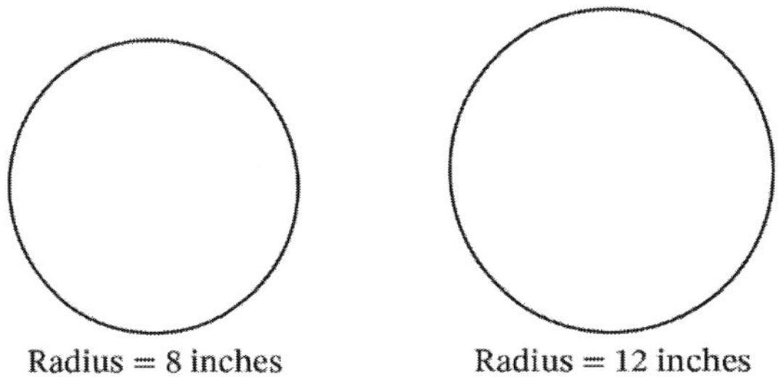

a. They are congruent.
b. They are similar.
c. They are neither congruent nor similar.
d. They are equal.

21. What is the value of $(5 \times 4) \div (2 \times 2)$?

a. 7.2
b. 6
c. 5
d. 4

22. $\angle AEC$ is a straight angle. $m\angle BEC$ is 45°. What is $m\angle AEB$?

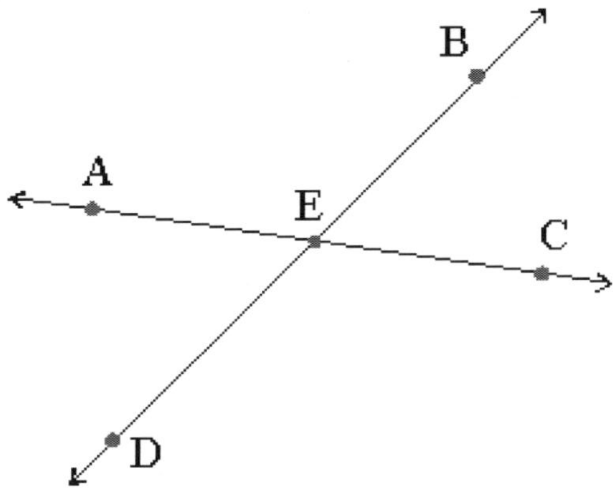

a. 90°
b. 115°
c. 135°
d. 180°

23. There are twelve inches in a foot, and three feet in a yard. How many inches are in five yards?

a. 20
b. 41
c. 75
d. 180

Refer to the following for question 24:

> Joshua has to earn more than 92 points on the state test in order to qualify for an academic scholarship. Each question is worth 4 points, and the test has a total of 30 questions. Let x represent the number of test questions Joshua answers correctly.

24. Which of the following inequalities can be solved to determine the number of questions Joshua must answer correctly?

a. $4x < 30$
b. $4x < 92$
c. $4x > 30$
d. $4x > 92$

25. Three children decide to purchase a car for their parents and share the cost. One gives $\frac{1}{4}$ of the cost, and another contributes $\frac{3}{8}$ of the cost. What portion of the cost will the third child have to contribute towards the car?

a. $\frac{1}{4}$
b. $\frac{3}{8}$
c. $\frac{1}{2}$
d. $\frac{5}{8}$

26. On his last math test, Sam got 2 questions correct for every 3 questions he missed. If the test had a total of 60 questions, how many questions did Sam answer correctly?

a. 12
b. 24
c. 36
d. 40

27. Find the value of $100 \div (9 + 1) \times 2$.

a. 5
b. 15
c. 20
d. 76

28. Which of the following represents the net of a square pyramid?

a.
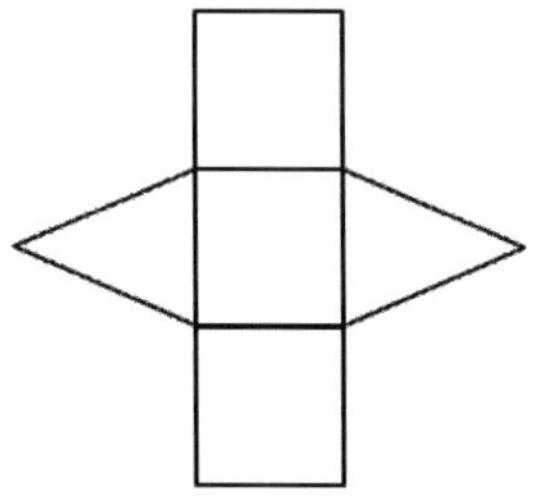

b.
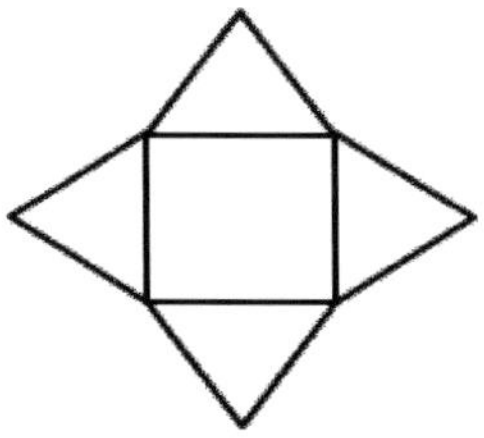

c.
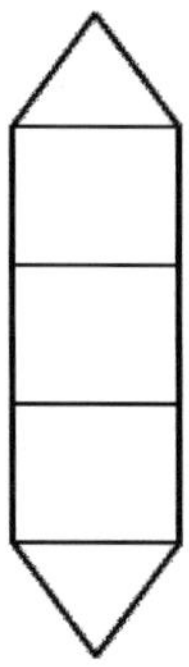

d.
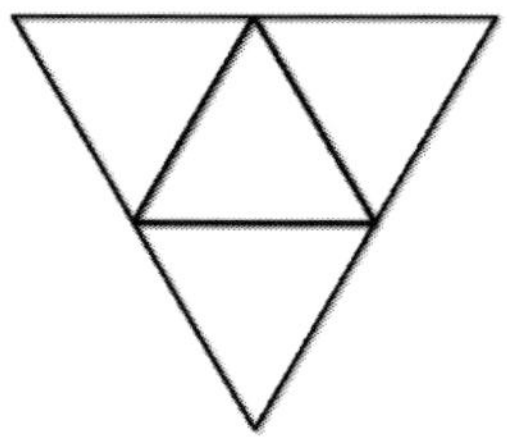

Refer to the following for questions 29–30:

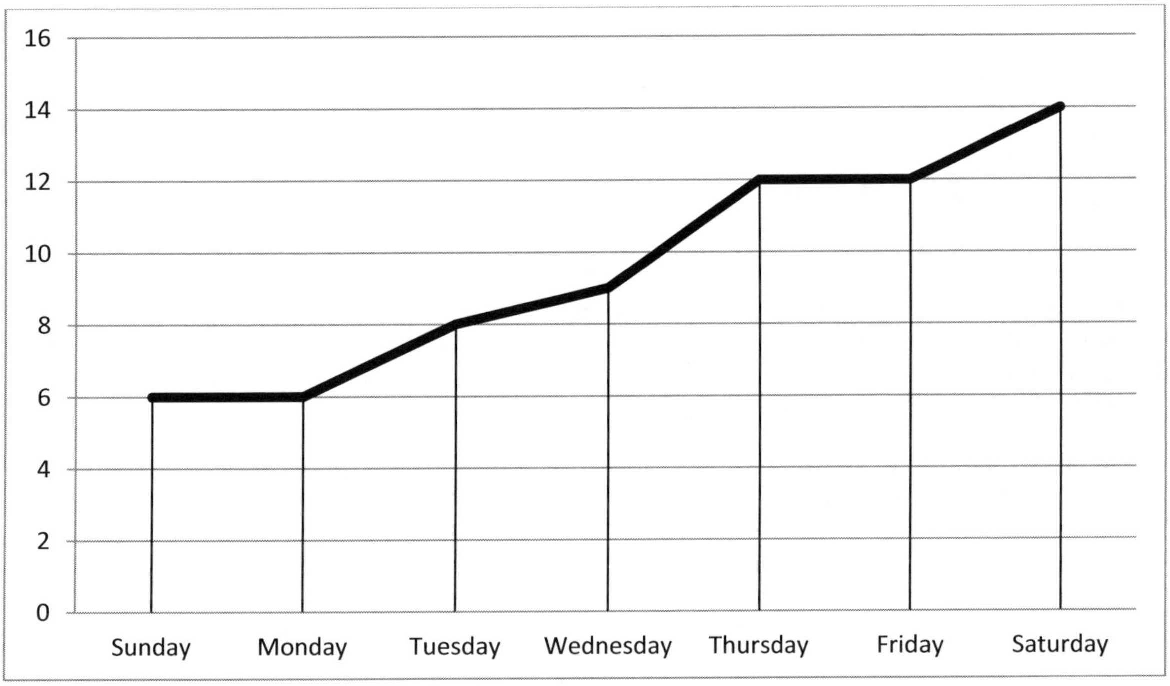

Every time Miguel gets quarters in change, he puts them in a jar. The chart above shows how many quarters he has in the jar at the end of each day during a particular week.

29. Which day did Miguel add the most quarters to the jar?

a. Monday
b. Tuesday
c. Thursday
d. Saturday

30. How many quarters did Miguel add on Monday?

a. 0
b. 1
c. 3
d. 6

31. What is the volume of the cube?

3

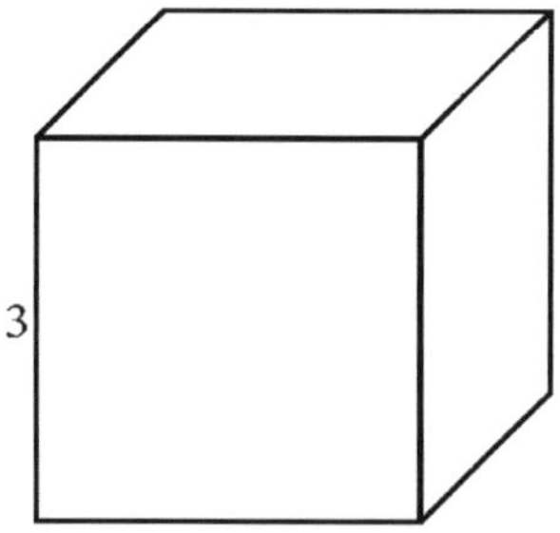

a. 9 cubic units
b. 15 cubic units
c. 27 cubic units
d. 33 cubic units

32. Candice is reading a map. She measures a distance along a road as 6.5 inches. If the scale of the map is such that one mile is represented as 2 inches, what is the real distance along the road that Candice has measured?

a. 3.25 miles
b. 4 miles
c. 6.5 miles
d. 13 miles

33. One inch is equivalent to 2.54 centimeters. How long, in centimeters, is a stick measuring 9.5 inches?

a. 241.3 centimeters
b. 24.13 centimeters
c. 12.70 centimeters
d. 3.7 centimeters

34. A man invested $150 in the stock market. During the first week, he lost $45. During the second week, he tripled his money. How much does he have at the end of the second week?

a. $105
b. $210
c. $315
d. $420

35. A raffle game has a single grand prize that will be drawn randomly from among all the tickets. A total of 500 tickets are sold. If a man buys 25 tickets, what is the probability that he will win the grand prize?

a. $\frac{1}{2}$
b. $\frac{1}{5}$
c. $\frac{1}{10}$
d. $\frac{1}{20}$

36. A dress is marked as 20% off. With the discount, the current price is $40.00. What is the price of the dress without the discount?

a. $32
b. $45
c. $48
d. $50

37. Three treasure hunters decide to split up their haul. The first treasure hunter gets $\frac{1}{3}$ of the treasure. The second treasure hunter gets $\frac{1}{4}$ of the treasure. What fraction of the treasure does the third treasure hunter get?

a. $\frac{1}{2}$
b. $\frac{1}{5}$
c. $\frac{5}{7}$
d. $\frac{5}{12}$

38. Felicia's new job requires extensive travel. If she is required to be out of town on business for 157 of 365 days this year, how many days is Felicia in town?

a. 208
b. 209
c. 218
d. 532

39. A reporter for a school newspaper surveys the students at the school to ask if they prefer chocolate, vanilla, or strawberry ice cream. Of the students who answer her question, 35% prefer vanilla, and 40% prefer chocolate. What percent of the students she surveyed prefer strawberry?

a. 15%
b. 25%
c. 35%
d. 40%

40. In the following figure of two intersecting lines, $m\angle B = 120°$. What is $m\angle A$?

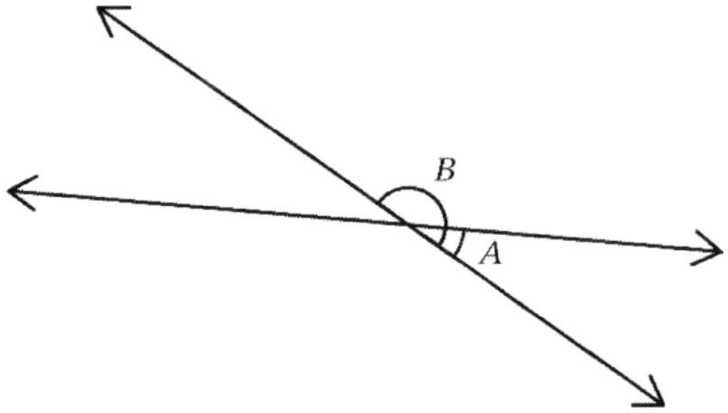

a. 40°
b. 60°
c. 90°
d. 100°

41. If x and y are positive integers, which of the following expressions is equivalent to $(xy)^{7y} - (xy)^{y}$?

a. $(xy)^{6y}$
b. $(xy)^{7y-1}$
c. $(xy)^{y}[(xy)^{7} - 1]$
d. $(xy)^{y}[(xy)^{6y} - 1]$

42. Consider two congruent circles of radius r, as shown in the figure below. If B is the center of the first circle, and C is the center of the second circle, what is the length of line segment $\overline{AD}$?

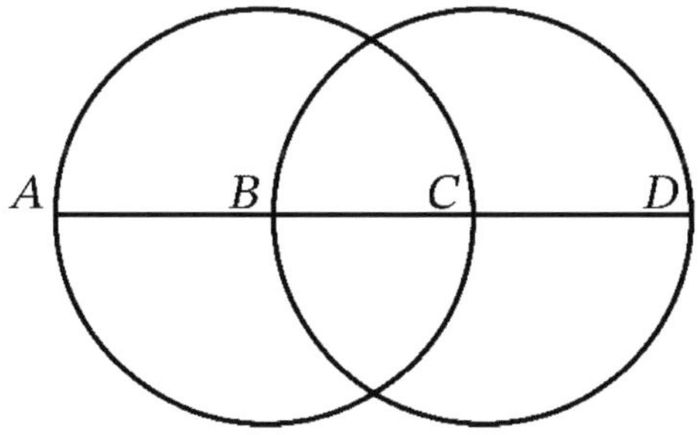

a. $2r$
b. $3r$
c. $4r$
d. $2.5r$

43. Which of the following relations represents a function?

a. $\{(2,9), (3,4), (6,8), (-1,5), (3,-1)\}$
b. $\{(8,7), (7,9), (2,1), (4,3), (3,6)\}$
c. $\{(-4,6), (2,1), (-4,-2), (3,8), (9,2)\}$
d. $\{(2,6), (6,5), (5,9), (2,0), (-3,1)\}$

44. There are 20 students in a classroom. Of the 20 students in the classroom, half are boys and half are girls. If all students handed in their homework, what is the probability that the top homework sheet belongs to a girl?

a. 50%
b. 40%
c. 30%
d. 25%

45. Which of the following is equivalent to $5^3 + 18 \div 3$?

a. 21
b. 37
c. $48\frac{2}{3}$
d. 131

46. A recent poll of a city of 25,000 showed that 70% of the adult residents are in favor of building a new community center. How many of the residents are NOT in favor of building a new community center?

a. 1,750
b. 7,500
c. 17,500
d. 23,250

47. A diver can hold his breath for two minutes underwater. After practicing for a week, he can hold his breath for 5% longer. How long will he be able to hold his breath after the first week of practice?

a. 0.1 minutes
b. 2.01 minutes
c. 2.1 minutes
d. 3.0 minutes

48. Which of these would best illustrate the percentage of a budget allocated to various departments?

a. Pie chart
b. Line graph
c. Box-and-whisker plot
d. Venn diagram

49. What is the mode of the following numbers: 14, 17, 14, 12, 13, 15, 22, 11?

a. 13.5
b. 14
c. 14.75
d. 16.5

50. What is the simplified form of $\sqrt{40}$?

a. $2\sqrt{10}$
b. $4\sqrt{5}$
c. 5
d. 20

51. A rectangular garden has a perimeter of 600 yards. If the length of the garden is 250 yards, what is the garden's width in yards?

a. 25 yards
b. 50 yards
c. 175 yards
d. 350 yards

52. A rectangle is twice as long as it is wide. If the width is 3 meters, what is the area in square meters?

a. 6 m^2
b. 9 m^2
c. 12 m^2
d. 18 m^2

53. What is the probability of spinning a 2 on the first try on the spinner below?

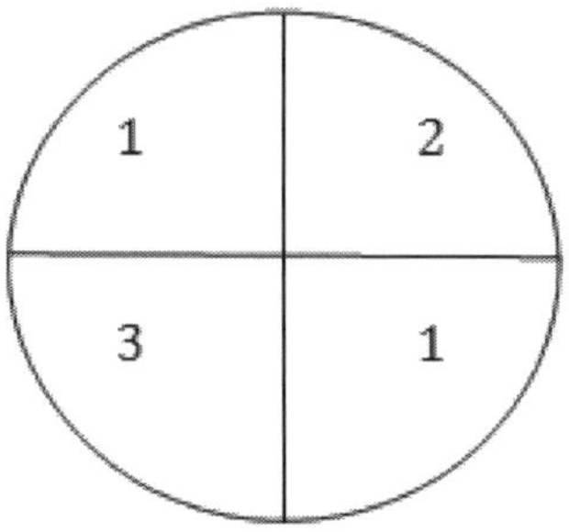

a. $\frac{1}{2}$
b. $\frac{1}{3}$
c. $\frac{1}{4}$
d. $\frac{2}{4}$

54. When three consecutive integers are added together, the total is 123. What is the value of the first integer?

a. 39
b. 40
c. 41
d. 42

55. Convert 250 centimeters to kilometers.

a. 0.0025 km
b. 0.025 km
c. 0.250 km
d. 2.50 km

56. A man owns a store. One week he sells 100 loaves of bread. If he sells twice as many loaves the next week, how many loaves did he sell in total?

a. 150
b. 200
c. 250
d. 300

57. How many feet are in 2 miles if there are 5,280 feet in 1 mile?

a. 5,150
b. 5,700
c. 10,560
d. 11,640

58. Which set of numbers are all multiples of 8?

a. 1, 2, 4, 8
b. 2, 4, 6, 8
c. 1, 9, 17, 25
d. 8, 16, 24, 32

59. Two women have credit cards. One earns 3 points for every dollar she spends. The other earns 6 points for every dollar she spends. If they each spend $5.00, how many combined total points will they earn?

a. 15
b. 30
c. 45
d. 60

60. Which of the following is a multiple of 3, 4, and 5?

a. 120
b. 150
c. 170
d. 190

61. It rained every day last week except Friday. If it rained twice as much on Monday as it did on Thursday, which of the following graphs could model the week's rainfall in inches?

a. 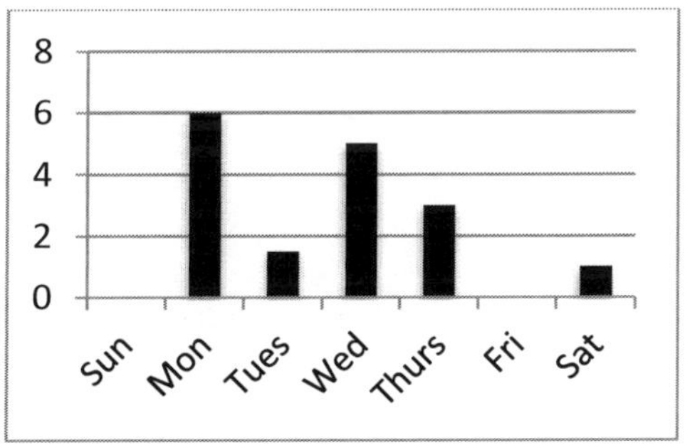

c. 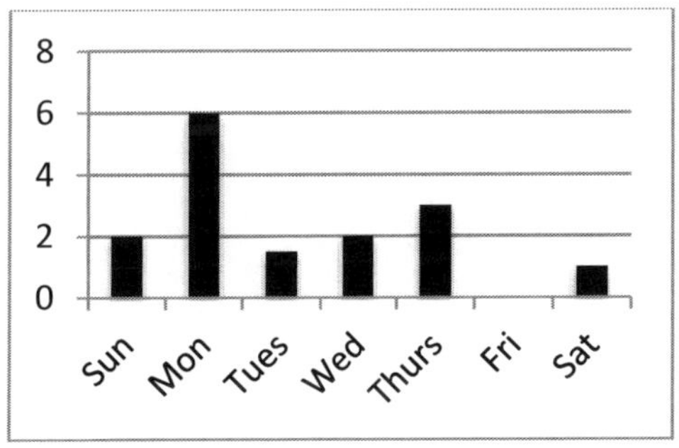

b. 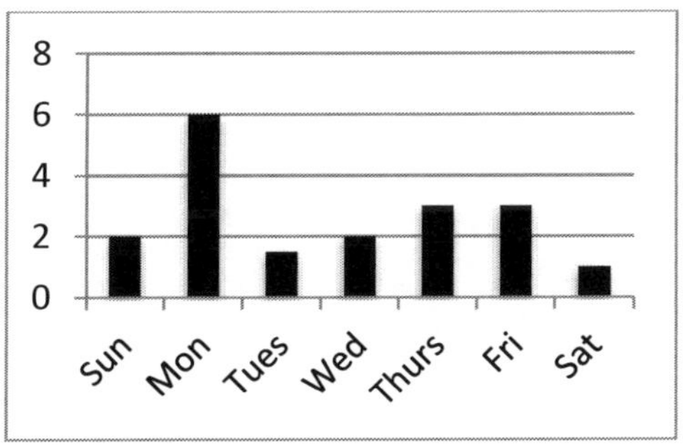

d. 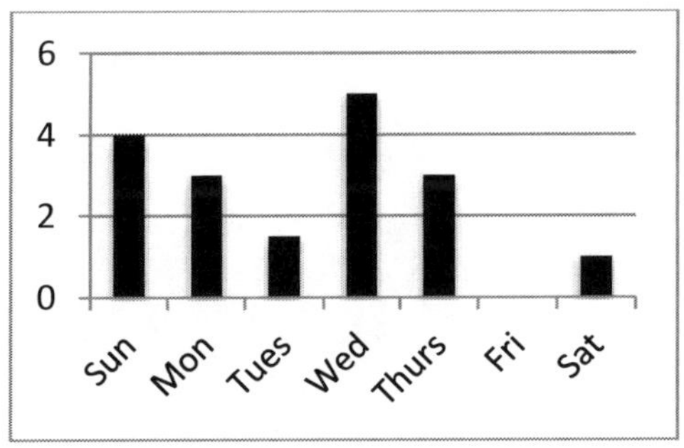

62. The two shortest sides of a right triangle are 6 and 8 units long, respectively. What is the perimeter of the triangle?

a. 10 units
b. 14 units
c. 18 units
d. 24 units

63. What is the value of r in the following equation?

$$29 + r = 420$$

a. $r = \frac{29}{420}$
b. $r = \frac{420}{29}$
c. $r = 391$
d. $r = 449$

64. Simplify the expression: $\frac{2}{3}(3-2)+\frac{1}{2}(2-4)$

a. $-\frac{1}{3}$
b. $-\frac{1}{2}$
c. $\frac{1}{2}$
d. $\frac{1}{3}$

Answer Key and Explanations for Test #2

Reading—Comprehension

1. D: After introducing its topic, the bulk of the passage describes the features that light produces on a photograph and the kinds of lighting that are used to produce these features.

2. C: The paragraphs describe the origins of photography and the early popularity of the portrait, then set the stage for the description of lighting methods by indicating the importance of good lighting for the portrait.

3. B: The quotation marks are used to show that the word was invented to describe the results of Schulze's process, but was later replaced by other terms to describe the outputs of photographic methods, and is no longer in use.

4. A: Light is being compared to a living thing, with characteristics of dynamism and animation, explicitly stating that a comparison is being made. (Light IS a living thing.) This is the definition of a metaphor, as opposed to a simile, in which the comparison shows two things to be similar, usually through the use of the preposition "like" or "as." (Light IS LIKE a living thing.)

5. C: The word is used here to describe something a photographer may do that is different from common methods, but that may be an element of his or her personal style. The point is that by showing technical competence with good lighting technique, the "mistake" may be presented as a deliberate flaunting of convention.

6. A: By using the noun "equivalent" to characterize the comparison, the author makes it explicit. Thus, it is a metaphor and not a simile. A simile is similar ("like" or "as") but not exact.

7. D: While all the other choices describe information that is included in the paragraph, its main purpose is to define a large number of terms.

8. A: The author uses this technique throughout the passage: placing a term in italics and using it in a sentence that describes what it means.

9. D: The sentence contrasts floodlights with strobes and implies that strobes, being more modern, do not share these negative characteristics of floodlights.

10. A: Both words refer to the person being photographed. The author uses them in this manner to avoid repeating the same word twice in one sentence.

11. C: The paragraph runs through the different kinds of lights used for portraiture, presenting the name of each in italics and in a sentence that describes or defines it.

12. D: The paragraph describes several ways of modifying the output of studio lights to "diffuse and soften" their output.

13. B: The passage describes the different types of studio portrait lights, modifiers, and the lighting features that they produce on a photograph. It does not go into detail on positioning (Choice D).

14. D: The only true statement about Ellis Island is statement III: The island was expanded using dirt excavated from the construction of the New York City subway system. Statement I is false.

According to Paragraph 1, Ellis Island is "within the shadow" of the Statue of Liberty. This means that it is close to the Statue of Liberty, but does not house the Statue of Liberty. Statement II is also false. Paragraph 2 states that the local Indian tribes had called it "Kioshk" or Gull Island, not Oyster Island.

15. B: To correctly answer this question, reread the sentence, replacing "portal" with each of the answer choices:

An island is a piece of land completely surrounded by water. This word does not make sense in the sentence.

A gateway is a passage or point where a region may be entered. This choice makes the most sense in the sentence and can replace the word "portal". This is the correct answer choice.

A boat is a vessel used to travel in water. This word does not make sense in the sentence.

A subway is an underground railway used in a large city. This word does not make sense in the sentence.

16. C: The author's style is giving facts and details, much like the style used in a history textbook. An immigrant's diary would be written in first-person and most likely give thoughts and feelings about the experience at Ellis Island. A business letter would have a date, salutation, and closing. A persuasive essay would use persuasive techniques to persuade the reader to adopt a particular argument or position, and a short story would be written to entertain, not inform.

17. A: Throughout its history, the island had different many names. To answer this question, first determine the current name of the island. The first sentence of the passage states the current name of the island, Ellis Island. You can infer from Paragraph 2 that the island's current name came from the name of a private owner, Samuel Ellis. All the other answer choices are true statements from the passage, but do not make a correct inference about the current name of the island.

18. D: The author most likely included all the names of the island to demonstrate to the reader the rich and varied history of Ellis Island. The author states that "Ellis Island had a varied history," just before listing and explaining the various names the island had throughout its history.

19. D: The passage describes the artistry of ancient Greek coins and gives the reasons why so much effort went into designing them.

20. B: The first sentence indicates that coins are utilitarian objects, and few are designed well enough to be worth considering them as anything more.

21. A: "Delectation" means to savor or to enjoy the flavor or beauty of something, in this case the design of the coins.

22. D: The word is defined in the second sentence of the passage.

23. D: The passage describes the coins as artistic objects, not simply because they were the first coins, but also because of the historical situation which is described, and which led to their being designed with great care and pride.

24. C: The text states that new coins were developed frequently, to commemorate battles, treaties, etc.

25. A: The text tells us that the designers were highly skilled and that they were so proud of their work that they signed it.

26. D: The sentence contrasts the artistic content of the coins with their use as a practical means of commercial exchange.

27. D: The text tells us that coin designs changed along with larger sculptures to reflect changing Greek artistic tastes.

28. B: The frequent need for new designs meant that the artisans who did the work had ample opportunity to perfect their skills.

29. C: The text tells us that the dated coins provide a dependable record of Greek artistic development.

30. D: Coins were developed as a means of commercial exchange, and the text tells us that this was their main use.

31. C: The passage describes several distinctive features of annelid anatomy and tells how some of them differ from other worms.

32. A: The term is defined in the text as an organization of the anatomy into segments.

33. D: The term is defined in the text between commas.

34. C: The text gives the example of feet specializing into grasping organs to illustrate this evolutionary advantage of segmental plasticity.

35. B: *Nematodes* differ from the annelids in the structure of the coelum. *Lumbricus* and leeches are both members of the Annelida.

36. D: The paragraph tells us that annelids can live in salt or fresh water and on land, and then gives examples.

37. B: The text states that the annelid coelom is formed later during embryology and probably evolved at a later time, as well.

38. D: The text indicates that the cerebral ganglia are enlarged, whereas the remaining ganglia in the nerve cord are merely repeating (unspecialized) units.

39. C: The text defines metemeres as segments, and discusses segmentation as the distinguishing feature of the phylum.

40. D: The text indicates that both nematodes and annelids possess a fluid-filled cavity which is involved in locomotion, or movement.

Reading—Vocabulary

1. B: Defaced means vandalized.

2. B: To desire something is to want something. Saying that a woman desired a new car has the same meaning as saying the woman wanted a new car.

3. C: If you say that you comprehend something, it is the same as saying you understand it. For example, saying you comprehend what another person is saying is the same as saying you understand them.

4. C: To wander is to roam. To say someone wandered around a mall is to say they roamed or walked around aimlessly, without a specific goal or destination in mind.

5. B: Describing somebody as courteous implies that they are polite and well-mannered. Polite and courteous both convey the same meaning.

6. B: To say something is sincere means that it is genuine or real. For example, saying someone showed sincere concern means that their concern was genuine, not fake.

7. D: Imminent means about to happen or soon-to-occur. It is often confused with its homonym, eminent, which means highly esteemed and admired.

8. C: When something is described as challenging, it usually means that it is difficult or demanding.

9. D: Constructed most nearly means built. If you say a home is constructed out of wood, for example, it conveys the same meaning as saying the home is built out of wood.

10. B: Spare means extra.

11. C: When somebody is described as intelligent, it usually means that they are smart.

12. C: Chuckled is a synonym for laughed. To say somebody chuckled or to say that somebody laughed conveys the same meaning.

13. D: To sprint is to run. Saying that somebody sprinted to their destination and saying they ran to their destination conveys the same meaning.

14. B: Brandish means to wave menacingly.

15. A: Something that is being observed is being watched. Binoculars are used to see things more clearly, so it makes sense that the man would be observing or watching eagles with binoculars.

16. B: Heritage can refer literally to an inheritance, or more broadly to a culture's traditions.

17. B: Constricted most nearly has the same meaning as narrowed.

18. D: To repudiate is to renounce.

19. B: Festivities are commonly known as celebrations. Attending festivities implies that you are attending a celebration or party.

20. D: Enhance most nearly has the same meaning as improve.

21. C: To say something is superior to something else usually implies that it is better.

22. A: Mulish is the adjectival form of the noun "mule," and means stubborn.

Language

1. B: The grocery list had four items on it; lettuce, tomatoes, cheese, and milk.

Error: semicolon

The semicolon between "items" and "lettuce" is incorrect. A colon should be used before a list.

2. D: No mistake.

3. C: How long were you engaged before you got married.

Error: period

The period at the end of the sentence is incorrect. The sentence is a question; therefore, it needs a question mark at the end.

4. B: There parents grounded Bill and Ben for a week.

Error: Incorrect word choice. Although "there" and "their" are pronounced the same way, the two words have different meanings. "There" is a location. "Their" is the possessive form of the pronoun "they" and it is the correct word to use in this sentence.

5. C: We worked on the project for day's and still got a bad grade.

Error: apostrophe

An apostrophe makes a word possessive, not plural. The proper form of the word in this case is "days."

6. D: No mistake.

7. B: The three textbooks you need is all in the bookstore.

Error: Incorrect word choice. The word "is" goes with singular nouns. This should use the word "are" instead.

8. C: We went with them to the fair last year, but their not going this year.

Error: Incorrect word choice. Although "their" and "they're" are pronounced the same way, the two words have different meanings. "Their" is the possessive form of the pronoun "they". "They're" is a contraction of the words "they are" and it is the correct word to use in this sentence.

9. C: Bruce Springsteen is often thought of as one of Americas' greatest songwriters.

Error: apostrophe

The apostrophe should go between the "a" and the "s" in America's. America is a collective noun, which means that it refers to a group of people, places or things. In the United States, the singular form of a verb is commonly used for a collective noun.

10. D: No mistake.

11. D: No mistake. Each of the choices are complete sentences. A complete sentence needs a subject and a verb. Of the choices, choice A is the most common to seem like a sentence fragment, but it contains a subject (she), a verb (ate), and even an object (two), though the object is implied and not explicitly stated.

12. A: George Washington, and Abraham Lincoln are our two most famous leaders.

Error: comma

There should not be a comma between "Washington" and "and". There are only two items in the list; therefore, a comma is unnecessary.

13. C: When I was in school, the Principal was a mean old woman.

Error: capitalization

Principal should be capitalized only when used as part of a name, such as in Principal Skinner.

14. A: The last house on my street was spooky old and creepy.

Error: commas

The list of adjectives describing the house needs to be divided by commas: "The last house on my street was spooky, old, and creepy." A comma should go before the conjunction *and* in a list of three or more items. A comma after the next-to-last item in a series is called a serial comma.

15. B: What town did your parent's grow up in?

Error: apostrophe

An apostrophe is used to make something possessive, not plural. In this case, the proper word would be "parents".

16. B: The letter stated that my application had been denied, which was written on formal letterhead.

Error: misplaced modifier

The phrase "which was written on formal letterhead" describes the letter, which means that phrase should be placed immediately after the word "letter."

17. C: When my brother said he was going to the movies, I said I wanted to go to.

Error: wrong form of "to"

"To" is a direction. The proper form of the word here would be "too", meaning "also."

18. B: The movie was totally sold out; which stinks.

Error: semicolon

The semicolon between "out" and "which" is incorrect. A semicolon should be used only between two complete phrases. "Which stinks" is not a complete phrase.

19. D: No mistake.

20. B: Steve loved jogging, hiking, and loved to bike.

Error: parallelism

21. A: Blogging has become a very popular form of communication in the future.

Error: tense agreement

The sentence begins in the past with "has become" and then ends with "in the future". All tenses need to be consistent. The sentence should read, "Blogging will become a very popular form of communication in the future."

22. D: No mistake.

23. A: "A mile isn't very far to run." said Steve.

Error: period

A comma should be placed at the end of dialogue, before quotation marks. The sentence should read, "A mile isn't very far to run," said Steve.

24. B: Principal Walters and governor Jones had a debate on television.

Error: capitalization

The word "governor" should be capitalized when it is part of a name.

25. D: No mistake.

26. D: No mistake.

27. B: When Sue went to the mall and bought shoes she also bought a dress and some sandals.

Error: This is a run-on sentence.

To be correct, the sentence would need to be broken up ("When Sue went to the mall, she bought shoes. She also bought a dress and some sandals.") or modified with a comma ("When Sue went to the mall and bought shoes, she also bought a dress and some sandals.")

28. A: Randall were very nervous on his wedding day.

Error: subject-verb agreement

Randall is one individual; therefore, the singular form of the verb, "was", should be used rather than the plural form, "were".

29. C: Two wrongs don't not make a right.

Error: double negative

"Don't" is the contracted form of "do not." Saying "don't not" is the same as saying "do not not", which is a double negative.

30. B: I went to the store, but I forgot to buy bread

Error: punctuation

There is no period at the end of the sentence.

31. A: George gets tired very easily especially when he is doing hard work.

Error: comma

There should be a comma between "easily" and "especially".

32. D: No mistake.

33. A: I went to the hospital to talk to the doctor on Grant Street.

Error: misplaced modifier

The hospital is located on Grant Street, so that phrase should be placed directly after "hospital", making the sentence read, "I went to the hospital on Grant Street to talk to the doctor."

34. D: No mistake.

35. C: I always enjoyed reading, writing, and to sing a song.

Error: parallelism

All items in a list should be structured the same way. In this list, that means the final phrase should be "singing" to maintain the "-ing" structure.

36. B: Her favorite subject in school was english.

Error: capitalization

"English" is a proper noun and should be capitalized.

37. A: I love movies, and television, but I like reading better.

Error: comma

There is no need for a comma between "movies" and "television."

38. B: He will go to the game, but didn't stay long.

Error: agreement

"Will go to the game" is in the future. "Didn't stay long" is in the past. Both tenses need to be the same. The sentence should read either, "He went to the game, but didn't stay long." or "He will go to the game, but he will not stay long."

39. B: If you give the dog it's bone, it might stop begging for food.

Error: wrong word choice

"It's" is a contraction meaning "it is." The proper word in this sentence would be "its."

40. D: No mistake

41. B: "Lazie" should be spelled "lazy."

42. D: No mistake.

43. A: "Wreked" should be spelled "wrecked."

44. D: No mistake.

45. C: "Tecnician" should be spelled "technician."

46. A: "Aparpment" should be spelled "apartment."

47. C: "Overwait" should be spelled "overweight."

48. B: "Their" should be spelled "there."

49. D: No mistake.

50. C: "Accepted" should be spelled "expected."

51. B: The sentence "The iPad is the most popular of the new tablet computers" introduces the iPad, which is discussed further in sentence 3.

52. A: The sentence "His most famous novel is probably *The Adventures of Huckleberry Finn*" introduces the novel, which is the subject of the remainder of the paragraph.

53. A: Volleyball is a team sport that follows the verb "to play," whereas individual sports like yoga follow the verb "to do."

54. D: The word "every" is a singular noun and should be followed by a singular pronoun. In this case, the only singular pronoun is "her."

55. A: The subject of this sentence, "a team," is singular, so the verb also should be singular.

56. D: In the original sentence, the modifier is placed too far away from the word it modifies.

57. A: This sentence contains an appositive that gives extra information and is set off with commas. Therefore, the subject ("Mr. King,") and the predicate (beginning with "created") should be a complete sentence that makes sense without the portion set off by commas. Choice B adds "he," which is not grammatically correct because "Mr. King" is already the subject. Choice C omits the second comma, not setting off the nonessential phrase "an individual of considerable influence." Choice D changes the meaning by saying that Mr. King literally gave his fortune to the community, but "give back" in the original simply means he contributed to the community in some way.

58. A: In this sentence, *whose* is the appropriate possessive pronoun to modify *opinion*. Choices B and D are grammatically correct, but they are awkward and change the meaning. Choice C combines two independent clauses with no punctuation, so it is incorrect.

59. B: Sentence 3, which is about the Yankees and their famous players, does not fit the overall topic of the Yankees and their World Series titles.

60. D: Sentence 5 relates a personal experience, which is off the topic of the controversial nature of climate change.

Verbal Skills

1. C: To secede is to split apart, the opposite of merge.

2. B: This analogy focuses on synonyms. Taciturn means demonstrating a reluctance to engage in conversation; reserved, or quiet or slow to present an opinion or emotion, is a synonym for taciturn. Loquacious means to speak a great deal, so talkative represents the best synonym for loquacious.

3. A: When somebody objects to something, it means that they disagree with it. A person who objects to the expression of a specific political opinion may be said to disagree with it.

4. C: We can diagram the first two sentences as follows: University Press > Institutes Press and Institutes Press < Academy Press, which tells us that University Press and Academy Press received more submissions than Institutes Press. Yet, we cannot be sure which publishing house received the most submissions.

5. C: A decade is made up of 10 years; a millennium is made up of 1,000 years.

6. D: A driver steers a truck as an engineer steers a train. (A) contains this relationship but in the opposite order.

7. C: We can diagram this sentence as follows: Dean > Ellie; Dean > Rob. In other words, Dean was born before Ellie and before Rob. We do not have enough information to determine whether Ellie > Rob is true.

8. B: Susceptible and vulnerable both mean open to harm or injury. Therefore, vulnerable is the best choice.

9. C: The other three answers can be either works of fiction or nonfiction. Autobiographies are nonfiction since they're inherently a representation of the author's life.

10. C: We can diagram this problem as follows: B<D, B<S. The problem does not give enough information to determine whether Steve has more than Denny.

11. A: Something that is soiled is stained or dirty. When somebody says their clothing is soiled, it is the same as saying their clothing is dirty.

12. D: Flagrant means overt, which is the opposite of obscure.

13. C: Bare most nearly means revealed.

14. A: We can diagram the first two sentences as follows: Kevin < Allen and John > Allen. Then, the third sentence claims that, John > Allen > Kevin which is consistent with the first two sentences.

15. B: Lucid means coherent, which is the opposite of confused.

16. C: We can diagram the first two sentences as follows: Samuel > James; Horace > James. These sentences do not give us enough information to prove sentence three, Samuel=Horace.

17. B: Jupiter, Earth, and Saturn are planets that orbit the sun; the moon orbits the Earth.

18. D: Copper, gold, and aluminum are all elements that can be classified as metals. Sulfur is an element that can be classified as a nonmetal.

19. B: When a strong opponent competes against an unlikely challenger, we sometimes call the unlikely challenger an *underdog* who will face the incredible odds of defeating the strong opponent. An attribute or characteristic of an underdog can be their *audacious* (i.e., confident or bold) attitude. Now, a *conspirator* is a person who is participating in a plan that has some illegal intent. So, a conspirator has the characteristic of being *elusive* (i.e., easily escaping capture).

20. D: The work of counselors, nurses, and lawyers call for working with people directly. The work of a novelist may include interviews or research with people, but their work is more solitary than the others.

21. B: Opulent means overtly luxurious or lavish, and affluent means to possess great wealth or material goods. Therefore, affluent is the best choice.

22. A: Discord means disagreement, while harmony means unity or peaceful coexistence.

23. D: Pinnacle means the highest degree or level, while base means the bottom or lowest part.

24. B: Sleet, snow, and rain are all different types of precipitation. Thus, precipitation is the category under which sleet, snow, and rain fall.

25. C: Inanimate most nearly means motionless.

26. C: Valuable means important, which is the opposite of worthless.

27. D: Compact means solid, which is the opposite of loose.

28. C: Complacent means smug or self-satisfied leading to a lack of concern, and nonchalant means calm, cool, and collected. Therefore, nonchalant is the best choice.

29. C: Outspoken most nearly means candid.

30. D: Impartial means to treat everyone equally, and equitable means to be fair or equal in treatment. Therefore, equitable would be the best choice.

31. C: We can diagram the first two statements as follows: John=tall and John=basketball player for his high school team. Just because John is tall does not necessarily mean everyone else on his team is. Therefore, we do not have enough information to prove that all the basketball players on John's high school team are tall.

32. D: Homage most nearly means tribute.

33. A: Pandemonium most nearly means chaos.

34. A: When it is said that someone is generous, it usually means they are giving and unselfish.

35. A: Aptitude means talent.

36. A: A residence is a place where a person lives; the term is often used to refer to someone's home.

37. B: Dictate most nearly means tell.

38. B: We can diagram the first two statements as follows: Jamie<Emily<Brianna. The third statement says that Brianna<Jamie, which is inconsistent with the first two statements, so it is false.

39. A: Flowers are gathered together in a bunch as hay is gathered together in a bale. The other answers do not reflect this collective notion.

40. D: Footballs, basketballs, and hockey pucks are all examples of sporting gear.

41. C: The other answer choices are general nouns. Choice C is specific noun. Cape Cod is a cape off the coast of Massachusetts.

42. D: Berate most nearly means scold.

43. B: Scissors are tools necessary for a haircut; a tractor is a tool necessary for harvest.

44. A: Refute means to disprove or prove wrong, so disprove is the best choice.

45. B: Endearment most nearly means affection.

46. D: As a reference at the end of a *book*, an *index* may be provided that contains key terms or phrases with page numbers where those terms or phrases can be found. So, we can say that an *index* is a part to the whole of a *book*. The comparison involves an *elegy* which can be a song or a poem that expresses terrible sadness for the death of a person. This *elegy* would then be a part to the whole of a *funeral* service.

47. D: Algebra is the study of arithmetic operations; biology is the study of organisms.

48. C: We can diagram the first two statements as follows: Allison likes foxes>beetles and Kelsey likes sheep>caterpillars. Foxes and sheep are both mammals and beetles and caterpillars are both insects; however, this does not mean that Allison and Kelsey like all mammals more than all insects. Since they could like certain insects more than certain mammals, there is not enough information to determine if Allison and Kelsey like mammals more than insects.

49. A: Aural refers to the auditory sense, or hearing.

50. A: Something paltry is cheap, base, or common.

51. B: Drummer is the only word in the list that refers to a human being. The rest refer to musical instruments.

52. B: A person who is said to be pallid is feeble or sickly.

53. D: Grapes are an ingredient of wine as wheat is an ingredient of bread. The other answers do not reflect this relationship.

54. A: This analogy is a matter of degree as starting with something basic and escalating to something more significant. The question begins with *jog* which is basic and general, and this is matched with *marathon* which is a 26.2 mile race that takes several hours to complete. So, the best choice is choice A which starts with a basic *hypothesis* (i.e., educated guess) and escalates to a *discovery*.

55. B: "Artist" is the general category that all the other items in the series belong to; painters, musicians, and dancers are all kinds of artists.

56. A: A year contains months; a foot contains inches.

57. B: This analogy focuses on antonyms. *Antipathy* and *sympathy* are opposites as *antipathy* means a strong feeling of opposition, and *sympathy* is the act of understanding another person's feeling or situation. You are given *convivial* which means sociable or cheerful, and you know that you are looking for the antonym of sociable and cheerful. So, *gloomy* means depressed or miserable, and this is the clear opposite to *convivial.*

58. B: This analogy focuses on synonyms. Arrive is a synonym for enter; acquiesce means to accept with some degree of reluctance. Thus, the most appropriate synonym would be accede, meaning to agree to a demand.

59. A: Foster most nearly means to care for, or nurture.

60. C: Active means energetic and lively, the opposite of inert.

Quantitative Skills

1. A: To solve, test each answer. Notice that in choice A the numerator has been multiplied by 3 to get 12. The denominator has also been multiplied by 3 to get 21. In choice B, the numerator has been multiplied by 4 and the denominator has been multiplied by 5. In choice C, the numerator has been multiplied by 3 and the denominator has been multiplied by 4. In choice D, the numerator has been multiplied by 4 and the denominator has been multiplied by 5. Therefore, choice A is the only correct equation.

2. B: A is a number in the thousandths. B, C, and D are in tenths. Three-tenths (0.300) is the largest of these choices.

3. B: If he has covered $\frac{1}{2}$ the distance after two hours, and $\frac{2}{3}$ the distance after four hours, and he does not backtrack, then the fraction of the distance he has covered after three hours must be between $\frac{1}{2}$ and $\frac{2}{3}$. To compare fractions, we can convert them to equivalent fractions with the least common denominator. The least common denominator across all the fractions is 60, so the distances become $\frac{1}{2} = \frac{1\times30}{2\times30} = \frac{30}{60}$ and $\frac{2}{3} = \frac{2\times20}{3\times20} = \frac{40}{60}$. Now convert each of the answer options.

$$\frac{2}{5} = \frac{2 \times 12}{5 \times 12} = \frac{24}{60}$$
$$\frac{3}{5} = \frac{3 \times 12}{5 \times 12} = \frac{36}{60}$$
$$\frac{3}{4} = \frac{3 \times 15}{4 \times 15} = \frac{45}{60}$$
$$\frac{4}{5} = \frac{4 \times 12}{5 \times 12} = \frac{48}{60}$$

Only $\frac{36}{60}$ is between $\frac{30}{60}$ and $\frac{40}{60}$, so $\frac{3}{5}$ is the answer.

4. D: The daily cost is $12 and the one-time cost is $20. If you rent the mower for x days, the total cost is $12x + 20$ dollars. This cost must be no more than $220, so you need to satisfy the inequality

$12x + 20 \leq 220$. Subtracting 20 from both sides yields $12x \leq 200$. Then, dividing by 12 gives you $x \leq \frac{200}{12} = \frac{50}{3} = 16\frac{2}{3}$. You cannot rent for a fraction of a day, so you can rent the mower for 16 days.

5. D: The triangle has three sides of length 10 inches, for a perimeter of $3 \times 10 = 30$ inches. The square has four sides of length 5 inches, for a perimeter of $4 \times 5 = 20$ inches. So, the perimeter of the triangle is longer than that of the square (since $30 > 20$) but is less than twice as long (since $30 < 40$).

6. B: To find the perimeter, we simply add up the lengths of all the sides. Proceeding clockwise from the upper left corner, pentagon A has a perimeter of $4 + 7 + 3 + 5 + 7 = 26$ cm, and pentagon B has a perimeter of $7 + 4 + 3 + 5 + 7 = 26$ cm. The two pentagons have the same perimeter.

7. A: Top row: $3 \times 5 = 15$ and $15 - 5 = 10$

Middle row: $8 \times 5 = 40$ and $40 - 5 = 35$

Bottom row: $6 \times 5 = 30$ and $30 - 5 = 25$

The missing value for x is 25.

8. D: To compare decimal numbers, we compare them at the most significant place, the leftmost place, at which they differ. All three numbers have the same digit, 2, in the tenths place, so we move to the hundredths place. In the hundredths place, $0.2\underline{4}$ has a 4, which is larger than the 3 in the hundredths place of both $0.2\underline{3}7$ and $0.2\underline{3}66$, so 0.24 is the largest number. To compare 0.237 and 0.2366 we next look at the thousandths place, where the 7 in $0.23\underline{7}$ is larger than the 6 in $0.23\underline{6}6$. So, 0.237 is greater than 0.2366. Thus, $0.2366 < 0.237 < 0.24$.

9. A: In choice A, a comparison of the digits in the tenths place shows that 0.2 is greater than both 0.0499 and 0.007. Then, a comparison of the hundredths place shows that 0.0499 is greater than 0.007. Choice B should read $-2 < 0 < 7$. Choice C should read $\frac{1}{3} > \frac{1}{4} > \frac{1}{5}$. Choice D should read $-10 < -4 < -1$. Therefore, the correct answer is choice A.

10. C: A number raised to the first power is multiplied by itself only once, so $16^1 = 16$. 2^8 is 2 multiplied by itself eight times, so $2^8 = 256$. Similarly, $3^3 = 27$. The smallest number of the choices 16, 256, 27, and 24 is 16, so 16^1 is the smallest number.

11. C: The table displays x- and y-values. Each y-value is the result of multiplying the corresponding x-value by 2 and then adding 0.5. When x is 3, y is $2(3) + 0.5$, which simplifies to 6.5. The missing value of y in the sequence is 6.5.

12. A: If Davis runs for x seconds at 9.4 feet per second, then his total distance from the starting point is $9.4x$, because distance = rate × time. If Christopher runs the same length of time at 8.6 feet per second, then his total distance from the starting point, including his head start, is $8.6x + 100$. Davis catches Christopher when they are the same distance from the starting point, namely when $9.4x = 8.6x + 100$. Solve the equation for x to find the time when this happens. First, subtract $8.6x$ from both sides to get $9.4x - 8.6x = 100$, which simplifies to $0.8x = 100$. Then, divide both sides by 0.8 to get $\frac{0.8x}{0.8} = \frac{100}{0.8}$, which simplifies to $x = 125$. That is, Davis catches up after 125 seconds.

13. A: The nth term formula for geometric sequences is $a_n = a_1 r^{(n-1)}$.

a_n represents the nth term in the sequence.

a_1 represents the first term in the sequence: 96.

r represents the common ratio: $\frac{1}{2}$.

n represents the position of the term: 10.

$$a_{10} = (96)\left(\frac{1}{2}\right)^{(10-1)}$$
$$a_{10} = (96)\left(\frac{1}{2}\right)^{9}$$
$$a_{10} = (96)\left(\frac{1}{512}\right)$$
$$a_{10} = 0.1875$$

The 10th term in the sequence is 0.1875.

14. B: The trick to determining if a number is divisible by 3 is to add the digits together, then if the sum is divisible by 3, the whole number is divisible by 3. Check each number.

$$46 \rightarrow 4 + 6 = 10 \rightarrow 1 + 0 = 1$$
$$555 \rightarrow 5 + 5 + 5 = 15 \rightarrow 1 + 5 = 6$$
$$2{,}018 \rightarrow 2 + 0 + 1 + 8 = 11 \rightarrow 1 + 1 = 2$$
$$8{,}912 \rightarrow 8 + 9 + 1 + 2 = 20 \rightarrow 2 + 0 = 2$$

Only the number 6 is divisible by 3, so the number 555 is divisible by 3.

15. C: Start with the first clue. A finished before B, but behind C.

This results in CAB.

D finished behind B, so CAB becomes CABD.

D finished before E, so E must be last: CABDE.

16. B: When figures are similar, their sides and their perimeters are proportional. So, the ratio of the perimeter, P, of the larger polygon to that of the smaller polygon is the same as the ratio of the length of the base of the larger polygon to that of the smaller polygon. That is, $\frac{P}{22} = \frac{9}{6}$, which reduces to $\frac{P}{22} = \frac{3}{2}$. To solve this proportion, we cross-multiply to get $2P = 66$ and then divide both sides of the equation by 2 to get $P = 66/2 = 33$ meters.

17. D: $a_n = a_1 + (n-1)d$ is the formula for the nth term of an arithmetic sequence.

a_n represents the nth term in the sequence.

a_1 represents the first term in the sequence.

n represents the position of the term.

d represents the common difference.

18. D: Suppose we use a to mean the length of the unknown leg (that is, the "other" leg), b the length of the known leg, and c the length of the hypotenuse. By the Pythagorean theorem, we know that $a^2 + b^2 = c^2$, so $a^2 + 24^2 = 25^2$. This simplifies to $a^2 + 576 = 625$, which gives us $a^2 = 625 - 576 = 49$. Taking square roots yields $a = \sqrt{49} = 7$. The ratio of the length of the hypotenuse to that of a is $\frac{25}{7} = 3\frac{4}{7}$, so the hypotenuse is more than 3 times as long as a.

19. B: Convert all the values into the same unit. For example, convert all values to meters.

The 4×100 meter relay race is 400 meters.

The 200-meter race is equivalent to 200 meters.

1 kilometer is equivalent to 1,000 meters. This means that the 5-kilometer race is equivalent to $5 \times 1{,}000 = 5{,}000$ meters.

From least to greatest, the distances are 200 meters, 400 meters, 5,000 meters. The shortest distance will take the least amount of time to finish, which is the 200-meter race.

20. B: The three interior angles of a triangle always add up to 180°, so we can calculate that $x = 180 - 23 - 101 = 56$. The four interior angles of a quadrilateral always add up to 360°, so we can calculate that $y = 360 - 90 - 123 - 93 = 54$. We note that $y < x$ (since $54 < 56$) but $x < 2y$ (since $56 < 2 \cdot 54 = 108$). Thus, $y < x < 2y$.

21. C: The sequence is arithmetic. Each term is the result of adding 0.4 to the previous term. The missing term can be determined by adding 0.4 to 16.3.

$$16.3 + 0.4 = 16.7$$

The missing term is 16.7.

22. D: To compare these lengths, convert them to the same units. In this case, inches is the simplest unit to use. There are 12 inches in a foot. So, 7 feet is $7 \times 12 = 84$ inches. Since there are 3 feet in a yard, 2 yards is $2 \times 3 = 6$ feet, which is the same as $6 \times 12 = 72$ inches. Since 72 inches < 75 inches < 84 inches, the lengths, from shortest to longest, are 2 yards, 75 inches, and 7 feet.

23. B: The values in the sequence can be expressed with a common denominator of 6. The values $-\frac{1}{2}, -\frac{2}{3}, -\frac{5}{6}$ become $-\frac{3}{6}, -\frac{4}{6}, -\frac{5}{6}$, respectively. Now the pattern becomes more apparent. Each value decreases by $\frac{1}{6}$ to generate the next value in the sequence. When $-\frac{5}{6}$ is decreased by $\frac{1}{6}$, the result is $-\frac{6}{6}$, or -1.

24. D: When comparing fractions, it is necessary to find common denominators.

$$\frac{49}{56} = \frac{7}{8} < \frac{6}{7} = \frac{48}{56}$$
$$\frac{108}{120} = \frac{9}{10} > \frac{11}{12} = \frac{110}{120}$$
$$\frac{26}{39} = \frac{2}{3} > \frac{9}{13} = \frac{27}{39}$$
$$\frac{7}{28} = \frac{1}{4} < \frac{2}{7} = \frac{8}{28}$$

Once all the fractions have been represented using common denominators, it is easy to determine which of each pair is greater since the greater is the one with the larger numerator.

25. A: Every side of a triangle must be shorter than the sum of the other two sides (this is sometimes called the triangle inequality theorem). Since the sum of 4 feet and 9 feet is 13 feet, the third side must be shorter than 13 feet. On the other hand, the 9-foot side of the triangle must be shorter than the sum of 4 feet and the third side. This means that the third side must be longer than 9 feet minus 4 feet, which is 5 feet. Consequently, the third side is between 5 and 13 feet long.

26. C: The sequence is arithmetic, so the nth term formula for arithmetic sequences can be applied.

$$a_n = a_1 + (n-1)d$$

a_n represents the nth term in the sequence. In this case, the value of the 15th term.

a_1 represents the first term in the sequence. In this case, 17.

n represents the number that is unknown. In this case, 15.

d represents the common difference. In this case, 2.

$$\begin{aligned} a_{15} &= 17 + (15-1)(2) \\ a_{15} &= 17 + (14)(2) \\ a_{15} &= 17 + 28 \\ a_{15} &= 45 \end{aligned}$$

The 15th term of the sequence is 45.

27. C: The Music Appreciation class has $\frac{1}{6} \times 108 = \frac{108}{6} = 18$ sophomores. The Databases class has $\frac{3}{20} \times 120 = 3 \times 6 = 18$ sophomores. The German Literature class has $\frac{3}{4} \times 28 = 3 \times 7 = 21$ sophomores. And the Calculus class has $\frac{3}{7} \times 42 = 3 \times 6 = 18$ sophomores. Thus, the German Literature class has more sophomores, 21, than any of the other classes, which have 18 each.

28. B: Compare each place value of every number to determine the largest number. Since there are all zeros in the ones place, move to the tenths place. The numbers 0.0236, 0.0339, and 0.099 all have a 0 in the tenths place, while 0.236 has a 2 in the tenths place. Since $2 > 0$, the number 0.236 is the greatest.

29. C: The sequence in the table can be described as $0.4x + 3$, where every y-value is the result of multiplying the x-value by 0.4 and then adding 3. The missing y-value can be calculated by multiplying 0 by 0.4, and then adding 3.

$$0.4(0) + 3 = 0 + 3 = 3$$

The missing y-value in the table is 3.0.

30. D: Geometric sequences have a common ratio. A common ratio is the amount that each term is multiplied by to generate the next term in the sequence. In this case, there is only one sequence that is geometric. Choice D, 324, 108, 36, 12..., is geometric because each term is the result of multiplying the previous term by $\frac{1}{3}$.

Choice A: 1, 8, 15, 22... This sequence is arithmetic. Each term is the result of adding 7 to the previous term.

Choice B: 20, 17, 14, 11... This sequence is arithmetic. Each term is the result of subtracting 3 from the previous term.

Choice C: 1, 2, 3, 4...This sequence is arithmetic. Each term is the result of adding 1 to the previous term.

31. C: The ratio of Josh's laps to Peter's laps is 3 : 5 or the fraction $\frac{3}{5}$.

A proportion can be set up to determine the number of laps that Peter runs, if Josh runs 18 laps.

$$\frac{\text{Peter}}{\text{Josh}} = \frac{\text{Peter}}{\text{Josh}}$$

In this case, $\frac{3}{5} = \frac{18}{x}$.

Solve for x using cross multiplication.

$$\frac{3}{5} = \frac{18}{x}$$
$$3x = 90$$
$$x = 30$$

Peter runs 30 laps.

32. C: The sequence is geometric. Each term is generated by multiplying the previous term by 2. Use the equation for geometric sequences to determine the 10th term, $a_n = a_1 r^{(n-1)}$.

a_1 represents the first term in the sequence, 3.

r represents the common ratio, 2.

n represents the number of the unknown term, 10.

$$a_{10} = 3(2)^{(10-1)}$$
$$a_{10} = 3(2)^9$$
$$a_{10} = 3(512)$$
$$a_{10} = 1{,}536$$

The 10th term in the sequence is 1,536.

33. C: Choice C, $a_n = a_1 + (n-1)d$, is the correct nth term formula for arithmetic sequences.

a_n represents the nth term in the sequence.

a_1 represents the first term in the sequence.

n represents the number of terms in the sequence.

d represents the common difference.

34. B: The y-values are the result of multiplying the corresponding x-value by 6 and then dividing the result by 2. For example, when the x-value is 4, the rule becomes $\frac{6(4)}{2}$ which simplifies to 12. The missing y-value is 12.

35. D: A sequence is arithmetic if each term is the result of adding or subtracting the same amount to the previous term. For example, choices B and C are arithmetic.

Choice B: 7.5, 32.5, 57.5, 82.5... each term is the result of adding 25 to the previous term.

Choice C: 17, 15, 13, 11... each term is the result of subtracting 2 from the previous term.

A sequence is geometric if each term is the result of multiplying or dividing the previous term by the same amount. For example, choice A is geometric.

Choice A: 2, 10, 50, 250... each term is the result of multiplying the previous term by 5.

Choice D is neither arithmetic nor geometric. This list of numbers has no consistent common ratio or common difference.

36. B: One way to compare fractions is to convert them to equivalent fractions with common denominators. In this case, the lowest common denominator of the three fractions is $7 \times 12 = 84$. Convert each of the fractions to this denominator: $\frac{1}{3} = \frac{1\times28}{3\times28} = \frac{28}{84}, \frac{2}{7} = \frac{2\times12}{7\times12} = \frac{24}{84}$, and $\frac{5}{12} = \frac{5\times7}{12\times7} = \frac{35}{84}$. Since $24 < 28 < 35$, it must be the case that $\frac{2}{7} < \frac{1}{3} < \frac{5}{12}$.

37. C: Substitute all known values into the nth term formula for arithmetic sequences.

$$a_n = a_1 + (n-1)d$$

The common difference is 4, so d is 4. The 16th term is 91, so n is 16 and a_{16} is 91. Isolate the unknown variable a_1.

$$\begin{aligned} 91 &= a_1 + (16-1)(4) \\ 91 &= a_1 + (15)(4) \\ 91 &= a_1 + 60 \\ 31 &= a_1 \end{aligned}$$

The first term in the sequence is 31.

38. C: Drew starts with $\frac{1}{2}$ of a pizza. He then cuts this portion into two equal shares. The result is now two pieces that represent $\frac{1}{4}$ of an entire pizza. Then he slices each of these quarters into two pieces. Now each piece is $\frac{1}{8}$ of the whole pizza.

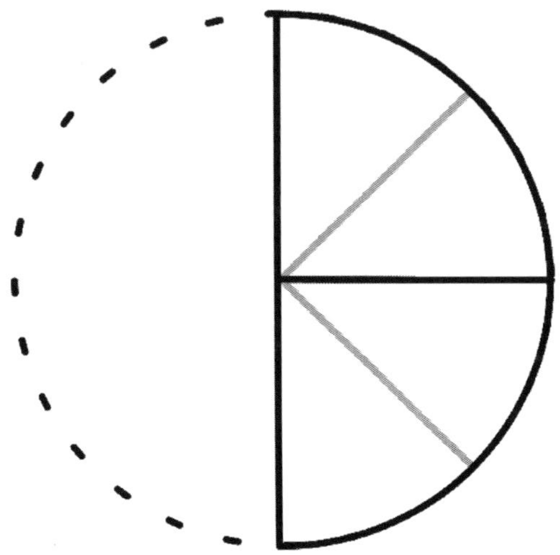

39. C: Start by converting all three values into the same unit. This will simplify the comparison process. Convert all three values into the smallest unit, pints.

1 quart is equivalent to 2 pints.

1 pint is equivalent to 1 pint.

1 gallon is equivalent to 8 pints, so $\frac{1}{2}$ gallon is equivalent to 4 pints.

The largest volume of liquid is 4 pints, which was Julie. Julie drank the most juice.

40. C: It is impossible to know whether angle A is the largest angle from the information given. For instance, the other two angles could be 60° and 56° (since $64° + 60° + 56° = 180°$), making angle A the largest. Or they could be 100° and 16°, making angle A the second largest. On the other hand, if angle A were the smallest angle in the triangle, then all three angles would be 64° or more, meaning that they would add up to more than $3 \times 64° = 192°$. This is impossible, since the angles of a triangle always add up to 180°. Thus, answer C is correct.

41. C: The volume of a cube is its edge length cubed (that is, its edge length taken to the third power). So, the volume of cube A is $2^3 = 8$ cubic feet, and the volume of cube B is $3^3 = 27$ cubic feet. Since $27/8 = 3\frac{3}{8}$, the volume of cube B is between 3 and 4 times the volume of cube A.

42. C: Write an equation to represent the given information.

$$x = \frac{1}{2}(4 \times 5 \times 6)$$

First, multiply 4, 5, and 6.

$$x = \frac{1}{2}(120)$$

Then, take half the product.

$$x = 60$$

So, the number that is half the product of 4, 5, and 6 is 60.

43. B: A calculator that cost you \$80 will ordinarily be listed for sale \$80 + 25% of \$80. Since $0.25 \times \$80 = \$20$, the usual price of this calculator is $\$80 + \$20 = \$100$. During the sale you take 10% off the usual price, reducing the price by 10% of \$100, which is $0.10 \times \$100 = \$10$. Thus, during the sale your customers pay $\$100 - \$10 = \$90$.

44. C: The scenario can be represented algebraically. Lynn has twice as many apples as Adam. This means that Adam can be represented using x, and Lynn can be represented using $2x$. The sum of Lynn and Adam's apples is 12, so the equation $2x + x = 12$ represents the scenario.

The equation can be solved for x.

$$2x + x = 12$$
$$3x = 12$$
$$x = 4$$

Adam has 4 apples; therefore Lynn has $12 - 4 = 8$ apples.

45. B: In a geometric sequence, terms are multiplied or divided by the same value to get the next term. In an arithmetic sequence, terms are added or subtracted by the same value each time. Choice B is the only sequence that is geometric. In this sequence, each term is multiplied by 2 to generate the next term.

Choice A: 6, 3, 0, 3, –6... 3 is subtracted from each previous term. Arithmetic.

Choice B: 4, 8, 16, 32... Each term is multiplied by 2. Geometric.

Choice C: 5, 9, 13, 17... 4 is added to each previous term. Arithmetic.

Choice D: 20, 17, 14, 11... 3 is subtracted from each previous term. Arithmetic.

46. C: We can solve the inequality $\frac{x}{9} > \frac{7}{11}$ by cross multiplying. The inequality will be true when $11x > 7 \cdot 9$, which simplifies to $11x > 63$. We divide both sides by 11 to get $x > \frac{63}{11} = 5\frac{8}{11}$. The smallest whole number greater than $5\frac{8}{11}$ is 6, so the answer is $x = 6$. Alternatively, we could rewrite the two fractions with a common denominator, getting $\frac{11x}{99} > \frac{63}{99}$, which gives us the same inequality $11x > 63$.

47. C: Write an equation that represents the given information.

$$x = 3(36 - 17)$$

First, subtract 17 from 36.

$$x = 3(19)$$

Then, multiply 3 and 19.

$$x = 57$$

So, the number that is three times the difference between 17 and 36 is 57.

48. A: Jane runs 300 meters in the first minute. Reduce this by 15% to determine the number of meters she ran in minute 2.

$$0.15 \times 300 = 45$$
$$300 - 45 = 255$$

Jane ran 255 meters in the second minute. Reduce this by 15% to determine the number of meters she ran in minute 3.

$$0.15 \times 255 = 38.25$$
$$255 - 38.25 = 216.75$$

Jane ran 216.75 meters in the third minute. Reduce this by 15% to determine the number of meters she ran in minute 4.

$$0.15 \times 216.75 = 32.5125$$
$$216.75 - 32.5125 = 184.2375$$

Jane ran approximately 184 meters in the fourth minute.

49. D: The ratio of blueberries to strawberries is 5 : 6. This means that for every 5 blueberries, there are 6 strawberries. Set up a proportion.

5 : 6 is proportional to b : 48, where b represents the number of blueberries.

This can be set up in fraction form: $\frac{5}{6} = \frac{b}{48}$.

Use cross multiplication to solve for b.

$$6b = 240$$
$$\frac{6b}{6} = \frac{240}{6}$$
$$b = 40$$

When there are 48 strawberries, there are 40 blueberries. There are $40 + 48 = 88$ berries altogether.

50. B: The volume of a box is the product of its length, width, and height, so this box has volume $V = 5 \times 4 \times 3 = 60$ cubic feet. The volume of a pyramid is one-third the area of the base times the height. So, the pyramid has a volume of $V = \frac{1}{3} \times 6^2 \times 5 = \frac{1}{3} \times 36 \times 5 = 12 \times 5 = 60$ cubic feet. Thus, the box and the pyramid have the same volume.

51. B: A 4-sided figure has 1 cut, resulting in 2 triangular pieces.

A 5-sided figure has 2 cuts, resulting in 3 triangular pieces.

A 6-sided figure has 3 cuts, resulting in 4 triangular pieces.

The expression $n-2$ can be used to represent this pattern, where n represents the number of sides of the polygon. This pattern can be used to determine the number of triangles formed within any polygon.

7-sided: $7-2=5$

8-sided: $8-2=6$

9-sided: $9-2=7$

10-sided: $10-2=8$

A 10-sided figure will contain 8 triangular pieces.

52. C: The distance formula tells us that the distance, d, between points (x_1, y_1) and (x_2, y_2) is $d = \sqrt{(x_2-x_1)^2+(y_2-y_1)^2}$. So, the distance between points A and B is $d = \sqrt{\left(5-(-2)\right)^2+\left(4-(-3)\right)^2} = \sqrt{7^2+7^2} = \sqrt{49+49} = \sqrt{98} = 7\sqrt{2}$. The distance between points A and C is $d = \sqrt{\left(1-(-2)\right)^2+\left(1-(-3)\right)^2} = \sqrt{3^2+4^2} = \sqrt{9+16} = \sqrt{25} = 5$. And the distance between points B and C is $d = \sqrt{(1-5)^2+(1-4)^2} = \sqrt{(-4)^2+(-3)^2} = \sqrt{16+9} = \sqrt{25} = 5$. Since $7\sqrt{2} > 5$, points A and B are farthest away from each other.

Mathematics

1. D: The equation may be solved for x by first subtracting b from both sides of the equation.

$$ax = c - b$$

Then, divide both sides of the equation by a.

$$x = \frac{c-b}{a}$$

2. B: Evaluate following the proper order of operations, starting with the operation inside the parentheses and then the exponent. After that, perform the addition.

$$\begin{aligned} 2^3+(4+1) &= 2^3+5 \\ &= 8+5 \\ &= 13 \end{aligned}$$

3. D: The histogram only shows that there are 8 trees between 70 and 75 feet tall. It does not show the individual heights of the trees, so this information cannot be obtained from the graph.

4. C: Will used the following calculations.

$$1\text{ bag of flour} \times \frac{5\text{ lb}}{1\text{ bag}} \times \frac{16\text{ oz}}{1\text{ lb}} \times \frac{25\text{ g protein}}{4\text{ oz}} \times \frac{1\text{ serving}}{50\text{ g protein}} \approx \frac{5\times16\times25}{4\times50} = 10$$

So, Will should divide the flour into 10 equal portions to equal the weight of chicken that would contain 50 grams of protein.

5. B: Simplify by using the order of operations. First, perform the multiplication, $(3)(12) = 3 \times 12 = 36$.

$$894 + 36$$

Then add 894 and 36.

$$894 + 36 = 930$$

6. B: The vertical-line test can determine whether a graph is a function. If any vertical line passes through more than one point at once, then the graph is not a function. A vertical line will cross a sideways parabola at two points anywhere beyond the vertex, so choice B is not a function.

7. B: First, figure out how many pieces of candy are in the bag before they are divided between the two friends.

$$26 - 8 = 18$$

Then, figure out how many pieces each friend will get by dividing by 2.

$$18 \div 2 = 9$$

Each friend will get 9 pieces of candy.

8. A: Lines 1 and 2 are parallel because alternate interior angles ($\angle C$ and $\angle B$) are congruent. If parallel lines continued into infinity, they would never cross. To intersect means that the lines cross. Bisect means that a line cuts another line or figure in two equal halves. Coincident lines lay exactly on top of one another.

9. B: Any number raised to the power of 0 is equal to 1.

10. D: The perimeter (P) of the quadrilateral is simply the sum of its sides:

$$P = m + (m + 2) + (m + 3) + 2m$$

Put together like terms by adding the variables (m-terms) together. Then, add the constants. This gives you $P = 5m + 5$.

In this problem, it seems that some of the variables do not have a number in front of them. However, when there is no coefficient, this means multiplication by 1. So, $m = 1m$, $x = 1x$, and so on.

11. B: First, calculate 30% of 3 inches.

$$3 \times 0.3 = 0.9$$

Then, subtract this value from the original height.

$$3 - 0.9 = 2.1$$

The grass is now 2.1 inches tall.

12. C: When the shirt is marked down by 25%, the cost of the dress is 75% of its original price. Therefore, the reduced price of the dress can be written as $\frac{75}{100}x$, or $\frac{3}{4}x$, where x is the original price.

When discounted an extra 30%, the dress costs 70% of the reduced price, or $\frac{70}{100}\left(\frac{3}{4}x\right)$, or $\frac{7}{10}\left(\frac{3}{4}x\right)$, which simplifies to $\frac{21}{40}x$. So, the final price is $\frac{21}{40}$ of the original price.

13. C: Simplify the expression using the order of operations.

$$(4+6)^3$$

Start by simplifying the part inside the parentheses.

$$(10)^3$$

Then, simplify the exponent.

$$10^3 = 10 \times 10 \times 10 = 1{,}000$$

14. C: To find the number, create an equation that represents the given information.

$$34 + n = 7 \times 6$$

First, multiply on the right side.

$$34 + n = 42$$

Then, subtract 34 from both sides.

$$n = 8$$

Therefore, the unknown number is 8.

15. B: The population is approximately 36,000, so one-quarter of the population consists of about 9,000 individuals under age 35. A third of 9,000 is 3,000, which is the approximate number of students in grades K–12. Since there are thirteen grades, divide 3,000 by 13. There are about 230 students in each grade. So, the number of fourth graders is between 200 and 300.

16. D: The net of a tetrahedron, or triangular pyramid, has four triangular faces. So only choice D can be folded into a tetrahedron. Choice A creates a triangular prism. Choice B creates a square pyramid. Choice C does not create a proper 3D figure because the triangular faces overlap.

17. A: First, add the Monday and Tuesday times together. That is, add 2 hours and 47 minutes to 4 hours and 56 minutes, to get 6 hours and 103 minutes. We can think of 103 minutes as 60 minutes plus 43 minutes, or 1 hour and 43 minutes. So, 6 hours and 103 minutes simplifies to 7 hours and 43 minutes. To find out how much time Bruce has left this week, we must subtract 7 hours and 43 minutes from the 12 hours he is allowed. This will be easier if we treat 12 hours as 11 hours and 60 minutes. Then 11 hours and 60 minutes minus 7 hours and 43 minutes is 4 hours and 17 minutes. That is, 11 hours minus 7 hours is 4 hours, and 60 minutes minus 43 minutes is 17 minutes.

18. D: Since one kilogram equals 1,000 grams, the conversion factor is 1,000. Since a gram is less than a kilogram, we divide by the conversion factor. So, 58.6 grams equal $58.6 \div 1{,}000$ or 0.0586 kilograms.

19. B: To find the amount of interest she will earn, multiply the amount of money in her bank account by 5% as a decimal.

$$\$450 \times 0.05 = \$22.50$$

Therefore, she will earn $22.50 in interest for the month.

20. B: Similar figures have the same shape but not necessarily the same size. Congruent figures are the exact same size and shape; they are equal. These two circles are similar.

21. C: Always perform the operations within the parentheses first before performing the operation between the parenthetical values.

$$20 \div 4$$

Now, divide 20 by 4.

$$20 \div 4 = 5$$

22. C: A straight angle is 180°. Subtract 45° from 180° to find the measure of $\angle AEB$.

$$180° - 45° = 135°$$

Therefore, $m\angle AEB = 135°$.

23. D: If there are three feet in a yard, then to convert yards to feet we just multiply by 3. So five yards is equal to $5 \times 3 = 15$ feet. Likewise, since there are twelve inches in a foot, to convert feet to inches, we just multiply by 12. So 15 feet is equal to $15 \times 12 = 180$ inches.

24. D: To determine the number of questions Joshua must answer correctly, consider the number of points he must earn. Joshua will receive 4 points for each question he answers correctly, and x represents the number of questions. Therefore, Joshua will receive a total of $4x$ points for all the questions he answers correctly. Joshua must earn more than 92 points. Therefore, to determine the number of questions he must answer correctly, solve the inequality $4x > 92$.

25. B: There are two fractions: $\frac{1}{4}$ and $\frac{3}{8}$. To answer the question, they must be added. The common denominator is 8, so express each of them as fractions with denominators of 8 and add the fractions.

$$\frac{1}{4} + \frac{3}{8} = \frac{2}{8} + \frac{3}{8} = \frac{5}{8}$$

With the first two people, $\frac{5}{8}$ of the cost of the car is covered. Therefore, to calculate the remaining portion of the cost of the car, subtract $\frac{5}{8}$ from 1 whole, or $\frac{8}{8}$.

$$\frac{8}{8} - \frac{5}{8} = \frac{3}{8}$$

The third child will need to contribute $\frac{3}{8}$ of the cost of the car.

26. B: The ratio of correct to incorrect answers is 2 : 3, giving a whole of 5 parts. Divide the total amount of questions by 5 to determine how many questions are in each part.

$$60 \div 5 = 12$$

Therefore, there are 12 questions in each part and 2 parts in the ratio designated to correct answers. Multiply 12 by 2 to find out how many questions he got correct.

$$12 \times 2 = 24$$

Sam answered 24 questions correctly.

27. C: Parentheses must be completed first. Here, $9 + 1 = 10$, so we can rewrite our expression as $100 \div 10 \times 2$. When dealing with multiplication and division, we must solve the operations in the order in which they appear, from left to right. Because division appears before multiplication, we must divide 100 by 10 before we multiply by 2. The quotient of 100 and 10 is 10, simplifying our expression to 10×2, or 20. Our final answer is 20.

28. B: The net of a square pyramid has a square base and four triangular faces. So only choice B can be folded into a square pyramid. Choice A creates a triangular prism. Choice C does not create a proper 3D figure because the triangle sides overlap. Choice D creates a triangular pyramid.

29. C: The line climbs the most sharply between Wednesday and Thursday, growing by 3 (from 9 to 12). Since the measurement is taken at the end of each day, we know there were 9 quarters in the jar at the end of Wednesday and 12 at the end of Thursday, so 3 quarters were added on Thursday.

30. A: The graph shows that Miguel had 6 quarters in the jar at the end of the day on Sunday, and there were still 6 at the end of Monday. So, he did not add any quarters that day.

31. C: The volume of a cube of side s is found using the formula $V = s^3$. In this case, since $s = 3$, the volume is $3^3 = 27$. The volume of the cube is 27 cubic units.

32. A: Since each mile is equivalent to 2 inches, divide the total number of inches measured by 2 to find out how far the true distance is in miles.

$$6.5 \div 2 = 3.25$$

Therefore, the real distance measured is 3.25 miles.

33. B: If one inch is equal to 2.54 centimeters, then we can multiply any measurement in inches by 2.54 to convert it to centimeters. To multiply decimals, we simply ignore the decimal points and multiply using the traditional algorithm. When finished, we count the total number of digits after the decimal point in each of the factors. The total number of digits after the decimal points in the factors should match the number of digits after the decimal point in the product.

$$\begin{array}{r} {\scriptstyle 4\,3} \\ \not{2}\not{2} \\ 254 \\ \times 9\not{5} \\ \hline {\scriptstyle 1\,1} \\ 1270 \\ +22860 \\ \hline 24130 \end{array}$$

Now, place the decimal 3 places from the right because there are 2 places after the decimal point in 2.54 and 1 place after the decimal point in 9.5. Therefore, the stick is 24.13 centimeters long.

34. C: First, calculate how much he had at the end of the first week by subtracting \$45 from the amount he invested.

$$\$150 - \$45 = \$105$$

Since he tripled his money the second week, multiply this value by 3.

$$\$105 \times 3 = \$315$$

The man has \$315 at the end of the second week.

35. D: Each ticket has the same odds of being the winning ticket, so the probability of a ticket being the winning ticket is $\frac{1}{500}$. If a man buys 25 tickets, his odds of winning are now multiplied by 25.

$$\frac{1}{500} \times 25 = \frac{25}{500}$$

We can reduce this ratio by dividing both numbers by 25.

$$\frac{25 \div 25}{500 \div 25} = \frac{1}{20}$$

Therefore, the probability that the man will win the grand prize is $\frac{1}{20}$.

36. D: If the dress's price is 20% off, it is $(100\% - 20\%) = 80\%$ of the regular price. So, the sales price of the dress, \$40, is 80% of what price? To find the answer, divide 40 by 80%, which is equivalent to the fraction $\frac{80}{100}$. Dividing by the fraction $\frac{80}{100}$ is the same as multiplying by its reciprocal, $\frac{100}{80}$. $40 \times \frac{100}{80} = 40 \times \frac{5}{4} = \frac{200}{4} = 50$, so, the original price was \$50.00.

37. D: The total must be 1, so the fraction that goes to the third treasure hunter is $1 - \frac{1}{3} - \frac{1}{4}$. To subtract these fractions, convert them all to fractions with the least common denominator, which is in this case 12.

$$\frac{12}{12} - \frac{4}{12} - \frac{3}{12} = \frac{8}{12} - \frac{3}{12} = \frac{5}{12}$$

Therefore, the third treasure hunter gets $\frac{5}{12}$ of the treasure.

38. A: The number of day's Felicia is in town is equal to the difference between the number of days in a year and the number of days she travels.

$$365 - 157 = 208$$

Therefore, Felicia is in town 208 days this year.

39. B: Since all students who answered her survey said they prefer one of the three flavors, the percentages must add up to 100%. Therefore, the percentage of students who prefer strawberry must be $100\% - (35\% + 40\%) = 100\% - 75\% = 25\%$.

40. B: The two angles form a straight line, so they are supplementary angles, which means they will add up to a total of 180°.

$$m\angle A = 180° - 120° = 60°$$

The $m\angle A$ is equal to 60°.

41. D: Remember that when you multiply like bases, you add the exponents, and when you divide like bases, you subtract the exponents.

$$(xy)^{7y} - (xy)^y = (xy)^y[(xy)^{7y-y} - 1] = (xy)^y[(xy)^{6y} - 1]$$

42. B: If B and C are the centers of the two circles, then both line segments $\overline{AB}$ and $\overline{CD}$ are equal to the radius r. The segment $\overline{BC}$ is also equal to r and represents the overlap of the radii of both circles. So, the total length of $\overline{AD}$ is the sum of these lengths, or $r + r + r = 3r$.

43. B: Choice B is the only relation in which there is not any x-value that is mapped to more than one y-value. Thus, this relation represents a function.

44. A: Out of the 20 students in the classroom, half are girls. That means there is a 1 in 2, or 50%, chance that the homework handed in will belong to a girl.

45. D: Following the order of operations, start by finding the value of 5^3, which is equivalent to $5 \times 5 \times 5$, or 125.

$$125 + 18 \div 3$$

Next, simplify the division.

$$125 + 6$$

Finally, add.

$$125 + 6 = 131$$

46. B: If 70% of adults are in favor of the new community center, this means that $100\% - 70\% = 30\%$ are not in favor. So, we need to answer the question, "What is 30% of 25,000?" Let n represent *what*, and replace the *of* with a multiplication symbol and the *is* with an equal sign. But first, we need to convert the 30% to a decimal. Remove the percent sign and move the decimal point two places to the left. Then we have $n = 0.30 \times 25{,}000 = 3 \times 250 = 7{,}500$. This means that 7,500 residents were not in favor of building a new community center.

47. C: First, calculate 5% of 2.

$$2 \times 0.05 = 0.1$$

Then, add this increase to the amount of time the diver could originally hold his breath.

$$2 + 0.1 = 2.1$$

The diver can now hold his breath for 2.1 minutes.

48. A: A pie chart shows the relationship of parts to a whole. A line graph is often used to show change over time. A box-and-whisker plot displays how numeric data are distributed throughout the range. A Venn diagram shows the relationships among sets. Therefore, a pie chart would best illustrate the percentage of a budget allocated to various departments.

49. B: The mode is the value of the term that occurs most. Of these terms, the number 14 occurs twice

50. A: Factor the expression.

$$\sqrt{40} = \sqrt{4(10)} = \sqrt{4(2)(5)}$$

Remove the perfect square from the radicand, the expression under the radical sign, by taking its square root.

$$\sqrt{4(2)(5)} = 2\sqrt{2(5)}$$

Finally, simplify the radical by multiplying.

$$2\sqrt{10}$$

51. B: The equation for perimeter of a rectangle is $P = 2l + 2w$. Substitute the perimeter and the length and solve for the width.

$$\begin{aligned} 600 &= 2(250) + 2w \\ 600 &= 500 + 2w \\ 100 &= 2w \\ 50 &= w \end{aligned}$$

Therefore, the width of the garden is 50 yards.

52. D: The area of a rectangle is calculated as the product of the width and length. If the length is twice the width of 3 m, then it must be 6 m long.

$$A = l \times w = 6 \times 3 = 18$$

The area of the rectangle is 18 m^2.

53. C: There are four equally possible places the spinner may land. The digit 2 is only present in one space, so the probability of landing there is 1 out of 4, or $\frac{1}{4}$.

54. B: The problem may be solved arithmetically or algebraically. To solve it arithmetically, divide 123 by 3, which yields 41. This is the middle integer. The other two must be $(41 - 1) = 40$, and $(41 + 1) = 42$.

To solve the problem algebraically, let the first integer be x. Then, since the integers are consecutive, $x + (x + 1) + (x + 2) = 123$, or $3x + 3 = 123$. Subtracting 3 from both sides of this equation yields $3x = 120$. Then, dividing both sides by 3 results in $x = 40$.

Using either method, the value of the first integer is 40.

55. A: 1 kilometer is equal to 100,000 centimeters.

$$250 \text{ cm} \times \frac{1 \text{ km}}{100{,}000 \text{ cm}} = 0.0025 \text{ km}$$

Therefore, 250 centimeters is equal to 0.0025 kilometers.

56. D: First, calculate how many loaves of bread he sold during the second week.

$$100 \times 2 = 200$$

Then, add the number of loaves sold during the first week to the number sold during the second week.

$$100 + 200 = 300$$

The man sold 300 loaves of bread in total.

57. C: Since 1 mile equals 5,280 feet, the conversion factor is 5,280. Since a mile is longer than a foot, we multiply by the conversion factor.

$$2 \text{ mi} \times \frac{5{,}280 \text{ ft}}{1 \text{ mi}} = 10{,}560 \text{ ft}$$

Therefore, there are 10,560 feet in 2 miles.

58. D: The multiples of any number are the number multiplied by any integer:

$$8 \times 1 = 8$$
$$8 \times 2 = 16$$
$$8 \times 3 = 24$$
$$8 \times 4 = 32$$

The first four multiples of 8 are 8, 16, 24, and 32.

59. C: First, figure out how many points the first woman will earn.

$$3 \times 5 = 15$$

Then, figure out how many points the second woman will earn.

$$6 \times 5 = 30$$

Finally, add these two values together.

$$30 + 15 = 45$$

Therefore, the two women will have a combined total of 45 points.

60. A: First, determine which numbers are a multiple of 3. For a number to be a multiple of 3, the sum of its digits must be divisible by 3.

$$120 \rightarrow 1 + 2 + 0 = 3$$
$$150 \rightarrow 1 + 5 + 0 = 6$$
$$170 \rightarrow 1 + 7 + 0 = 8$$
$$190 \rightarrow 1 + 9 + 0 = 10$$

Only 3 and 6 are divisible by 3, so the numbers 120 and 150 are multiples of 3. Now, determine which numbers are a multiple of 4. For a number to be a multiple of 4, the last two digits must be evenly divisible by 4.

$$120 \rightarrow 20 \div 4 = 5$$
$$150 \rightarrow 50 \div 4 = 12.5$$

The only number that is a multiple of 4 is 120. Since this number ends in a 0, it is also a multiple of 5.

61. C: We are looking for a graph with two key pieces of information: rainfall every day except Friday, and an amount of rain on Monday double the rain on Thursday. Answer choice A is incorrect because it shows no rain on Sunday. Answer choice B is incorrect because it shows rain on Friday. Answer choice D is incorrect because the amount of rain on Monday is equal to the amount of rain on Thursday. Only answer choice C is correct because it shows no rain on Friday, 6 inches on Monday, and 3 inches on Thursday.

62. D: The longest side of a right triangle, called the hypotenuse, H, can be calculated using the Pythagorean theorem, together with the lengths of the other two sides, which are given as 6 and 8 units.

$$\begin{aligned} H^2 &= (S_1)^2 + (S_2)^2 \\ H^2 &= 6^2 + 8^2 \\ H^2 &= 36 + 64 \\ H^2 &= 100 \\ \sqrt{H^2} &= \sqrt{100} \\ H &= 10 \end{aligned}$$

Therefore, using $H = 10$, the perimeter, P, can be calculated as follows: $P = 10 + 6 + 8 = 24$. The perimeter of the triangle is 24 units.

63. C: Subtract 29 from both sides of the equation to isolate r.

$$29 + r = 420$$
$$29 + r - 29 = 420 - 29$$
$$r = 391$$

The value of r is 391.

64. A: Evaluate the expression using the order of operations. Start by simplifying the operations inside parentheses.

$$\frac{2}{3}(3-2)+\frac{1}{2}(2-4)$$
$$\frac{2}{3}(1)+\frac{1}{2}(-2)$$

Then, simplify the multiplication.

$$\frac{2}{3}-\frac{2}{2}$$

Next, simplify the fraction $\frac{2}{2}$.

$$\frac{2}{3}-1$$

Since we are subtracting fractions, change 1 to the equivalent fraction $\frac{3}{3}$ so the two fractions have the same denominator, and subtract the two fractions.

$$\frac{2}{3}-\frac{3}{3}=-\frac{1}{3}$$

It's Your Moment, Let's Celebrate It!

Share your story @mometrixtestpreparation